M000014928

The Last Tackle

James G. Wallgren

Copyright © 2020 by James G. Wallgren

All rights reserved. This book or any portion thereof may not be reproduced or used in any manner whatsoever without the express written permission of the publisher except for the use of brief quotations in a book review.

Printed in the United States of America
First Printing, 2020
A3J Media LLC
a3jmedia@yahoo.com

This is a true story. I have tried to recreate events, locales and conversations from my memories of them. In order to maintain their anonymity in some instances I have changed the names of individuals and places, and I may have changed some identifying characteristics and details such as physical properties, occupations and places of residence.

I dedicate this book to individuals and their families struggling with spinal cord injuries. Let my story of forty years as a C5/6 quadriplegic give you hope that life can be just as fulfilling and joyful as ever.

A special thank you to my father for his selfless dedication to his son when he needed you most.

CONTENTS

Acknowledgment

To my parents – For the caring and understanding that prepared me for life's challenges. For holding me accountable, and allowing me to live the most grateful life possible. For just being present in my life. For teaching me compassion, respect and consideration for others as a foundation from an early age. I could never repay you for all that you have done over the years. To a mother in whom I could always confide my thoughts and feelings. To a father who is also a mentor; someone to whom I aspire. I will always love you both.

To my siblings – Given the disruption to our family life, I know it must have been difficult to take the back seat. I know I played a big role in that, and I will forever regret how painful it must have been for both of you.

You both stepped up in different ways when I was not able to, and for that, I am forever grateful.

To my children – Both of you have brought so much joy and happiness into my life. You two have taught me so much about living the best possible life. Please know that I have done everything I possibly could to prepare you for the joy, disappointments and realities of this world. Your life will have many twists and turns, some good and some not. Sometimes your choices will work out and sometimes they won't. That's okay; that's what's living is all about. You are the inspiration for this book. I will always love you both.

To my wife – What an amazing trip we embarked on some 30-plus years ago. You have been my lighthouse when at times I've seemed lost at sea. You are a point of reference that guides me and gives me comfort when I need it most. You understand me better than I know myself sometimes. Your compassion and dedication towards me and the kids is admirable. How you view and treat others without filters is frankly inspiring. We have been through a lot together. I am so lucky to have you as a partner and wife. I love you so much.

CHAPTER 1

When parents first hold their newborn children, they don't think about the roads their children will travel as they grow. They don't think about the "What Ifs". Rather, they enjoy the moment, and the bonding process with the little miracle wrapped snugly in their arms. Most parents want to protect their children from harm; sometimes, that's not possible. All the love in the world can't stop fate, which at times runs over us like a speeding train. It can be a tough lesson for any parent when tragedy strikes. My parents didn't escape tough lessons learned, and nor did we, their children.

My mother was a television personality in 1964. She had her own segment on a Charleston, South Carolina station, *The Girl on the Go*. She met my father through mutual friends. Dad was a captain in the United States Air Force and stationed at Charleston. He was a navigator in a C-130 squadron that flew all over the world, carrying cargo and troops. There was probably no place in the world my father hadn't flown over.

By 1964, the situation in Vietnam was really gearing up. Three North Vietnamese torpedo boats attacked the *USS Maddox*, prompting Congress to fully initiate the war against North Vietnam. My father was in Vietnam and flew dangerous missions. He lost several friends in the churning cauldron of Southeast Asia.

While he was back in Charleston, one of my father's squadron buddies was dating a girl who knew my mother. My parents were introduced, and they hit it off. My dad was a farm kid from Oklahoma and was adept at many things. My mother had been raised in the coal mining regions of West Virginia. With his career keeping him so busy—my dad said he never had time for TV then—he was unaware of my mother's TV show;

it didn't matter. She won his heart regardless, and they married in that pivotal year in American history. It was a time when the Beatles held the top five slots on Billboard, and when the Civil Rights Act was signed, the country was thrown into turmoil.

My parents weathered the storm. I was born in the spring of 1965, and immediately, through no effort of my own, landed in the record books. At twenty-five inches long, I was the tallest baby ever born in that hospital. I had inherited long legs from my mother, and a long torso from my father. I kept growing, and eventually topped out at 6'7".

Due to the nature of my father's job, he was gone for weeks at a time. During the first two years of my life, he wasn't home much at all; yet, we ended up being extremely close. After spending nearly three years in Vietnam and completing a six-year stint in the US Air Force, he resigned his commission in the spring of 1967. My dad had lost several friends in combat, and the war was worsening. It was a good time to leave. He ventured out on a new career that had the family on the move.

We landed in Garland, Texas, an interesting place to be for my Oklahoman dad. He started work with a pest control company, and our family moved a few more times. From Garland, we went to Waco, where my sister was born in 1968. Then we headed to San Antonio, eventually going back to Garland where we put down roots and I ended up spending all my school years. Robbie, my older brother, suffered from all the moves. He was an August baby, and a lot younger than his classmates. I think that in retrospect, my parents wished that they had held him back a year.

Robbie had been at a disadvantage from the start. Three years older than me, he went through several school systems because of our moves. Those formidable years for him, and it was hard for him to feel secure, or to have friends. Just when he found a good group of friends, the family moved again, primarily for financial reasons. My sister and I were fortunate that we got to stay put during our school years—it made a difference.

Robbie and I had the typical brotherly relationship. Sometimes we could be the best of friends; other times, we were the best of rivals—although I always knew he had my back.

My sister, Mendy, and I usually got along well. She was a pure girl: into piano, dance, and all things girls do. Although for the most part we got along, there were times when having a little sister could be a pain. My best friend, Randy, also had a kid sister and we would often have to watch the girls while our parents were away, or busy.

In the summers, Randy and I would want to go swimming at the community pool, or go to the park to hang out. My mother would say, "Well, you take your sister with you and watch out for her." What could I do? Inevitably, Mendy came along, and Randy's sister did too.

I remember the times we'd go to Holford Park. Randy and I wanted to chase girls, and we certainly didn't want our little sisters tagging along. We told them to get lost, and where we would meet up later. It was a different time then ... You could send your kids to a park, and not worry about their safety. It was also a time when nobody locked their front doors.

When I was in kindergarten, I had my first crush on a girl. Well, at the time it seemed like a crush. Her name was Kitsy (I had never heard that name before) and she was my kindergarten teacher's daughter. It wasn't until I got into middle school, seventh grade to be exact, when my first big crush hit. Between classes, as kids were headed towards their next room, she and I would walk down the crowded hallways, holding hands, which was kind of a big deal back then.

There were columns every few feet in the hall—an obstacle course of sorts. Well, I liked to kiss the girl as we walked. One time, we kept kissing until I turned my head just before I smacked right into one of the columns! *Wham!* I was knocked down big time. Talk about embarrassing! At that age, it was important to act cool, to be cool, and to have everybody think you *were* cool! I had failed miserably. There I was—the big guy in the hall—a tall kid trying to be impressive. I got up and felt like I was two inches tall. Lesson learned. But I was a tough kid, resilient by nature; most of us guys were rugged back then.

We'd do all sorts of wild things, and some of those things could have left us seriously injured. Evel Knievel was popular then, and my friends and I would try all sorts of stunts to be like him, such as using homemade ramps to jump our bikes over garbage cans. In our minds, we were just like Evel Knievel—flying high, and scoring a perfect landing. I used to tell people that I couldn't believe I didn't break my neck. Kids would also line up, and some of us would jump over kids. Sometimes, a competition arose where a guy would say, "I'll jump over five kids!" And we'd try to do it. A mother of one of my friends stopped us from jumping over kids, so then we went back to jumping trash cans.

A friend of mine had a trampoline and I often went over to his house with some other kids. We'd put one kid on the trampoline and then we'd get on the roof of the house and jump off. The object was to jump just right so that we'd knock the other kid off the trampoline. One day, we jumped off the roof onto the trampoline, knocking the kid who stood on it clear off into the fence. He was doubled over in pain, but he lived to tell about it! Amazing!

Usually, by the time I got home, I was covered in dirt from head to toe—testimony to a great day of hard play. I was so dirty that the bathwater was black when I got out. In those days, the boys in the neighborhood really lived the "boys will be boys!" maxim. It was a blast. Looking back, I don't understand how we avoided being killed. Yes, we were rugged all right.

Living in a middle-class neighborhood, we all had struggles. Families worked hard to make ends meet. My family struggled to keep the lights on and the bills paid. In 1975, a loaf of bread cost about 28 cents! Gas was 57 cents per gallon and a gallon of milk cost $1.40. Looking back, those seem like such small amounts compared to today's prices, but when the average yearly income was a little over $9000, it made for rough times.

The economy was stagnant; still, we made our own fun. We didn't have the distractions—the electronic temptations—that kids have today. The outdoors called and we always responded.

Some of the best times I had were with my family. Driving as if he was still flying missions in his squadron, my dad would take us on road trips for his sales job.

We'd travel for what seemed like an eternity, seeing the country and historic places. Pit stops were rare, causing our bladders great stress. My dad would pass a bottle back to Robbie and me, but Mendy and my mother weren't as fortunate. My mother would finally speak up and demand that Dad stop at a gas station. I think my sister developed a huge bladder because of those trips.

When we got to the town where Dad had business, we would check into a motel. My father would go make his sales call while Mom and the rest of us stayed behind. It was pool time! None of my friends had pools, so at home, we had to go to the community pool. However, it was a blast to go traveling because we could hang out at the motel pool all day until Dad came back. Then, it was off to go sightseeing! I learned a great deal about our country and our history on those road trips. Most of my friends never left Texas, so I had the advantage on them. Sure, we were middle-class, but those trips were worth millions! From coast to coast, we had the best education possible.

Spring and summer also meant playing sports. I played all sports, and especially loved to play baseball. I can still remember the smell of the fresh cut grass in the outfield. At the beginning of the season, the infields were composed of dirt. In our area of Texas, we had black dirt gumbo—a type of soil that was great for planting crops, but not so good for fielding ground balls. It would clot up and had to be dragged to smooth it out. To do this, we would drag a converted wood pallet or bedspring weighed down by rocks, or sometimes kids behind a car or truck. The dust would fly high in the air, giving off an earthy smell and leaving no doubt that it was baseball season.

My dad was a big help when it came to baseball. He'd gotten a baseball scholarship to Oklahoma State, where he played for a year. He then got an academic scholarship and transferred to a school in Ada,

Oklahoma, which was nearer to his home. He was the first in his family to get a college degree, which was an incredible testimony to his hard work. A poor farm kid who lived in a dirt floor house had made it big! He was my hero!

When it came time for Little League, my dad was right there helping. If a team was missing a coach, he would step up and take over. He was great with kids and they looked up to Mr. Wallgren! I often overheard kids talk about my dad, saying he was a cool guy, a great coach. To me, he was all that and more! There were even times when he coached my team—another lesson to be learned there. That didn't always go well for me, especially when I had a bad day on the field. Some kids would make cracks like, "You're only playing cuz you're the coach's son!" I have to admit that stung a bit.

I remember having some horrible games. At the time, I played centerfield and loved to run and catch fly balls, trying to judge where they'd be. Sometimes balls would go between my legs as I was trying to scoop them up. Those were the days that made me shake my head.

I certainly didn't need anybody to get after me when I didn't play well. Being very critical of my abilities or inabilities—I did enough of that myself. I would spend time analyzing what I was doing wrong and force myself to go back to the basics. It's the first time I remember being conscious of having to prove myself to others. As the coach's son, I had to be that much better. This lesson served me well when I went to find work, and after some life-changing events.

Having a wretched day at the plate never felt good, especially when I struck out each time at bat. One day, my dad came up to me after one of those tough games. He put his hand on my shoulder and told me, "Great game!"

I looked at him and said, "I don't know what game you were watching, but I didn't have a great game!" It was horrible, yet my dad made me realize that even Mickey Mantle struck out—a lot! Moreover, you can't hit homers unless you take your swings. The secret was to keep swinging and improving.

My dad always made me feel better with his words of encouragement. Over the years, I grew closer to him, and we got to the point where we could finish each other's sentences. Those times with Dad are irreplaceable. When it came time for me to be tried by fire, our shared experiences formed such a strong foundation because I remembered my dad's fine example. Little did I know that something very challenging was on the horizon, and that later, his words would still hold merit in some very dark times.

CHAPTER 2

About the same time that I started Little League, I began to have trouble seeing the ball, and in school, whatever was written on the blackboard was a blur to me. Eye exams weren't the norm back then; in fact, they were considered a luxury. But my teacher figured out that I might be having eye problems because I couldn't see the blackboard clearly, so she suggested an eye exam. Luxury or not, it needed to be done.

The eye test revealed that I was myopic, and to my dismay—just as to most kids' dismay—I ended up having to wear glasses. Glasses in general weren't cool at all, especially my black, horned-rimmed pair. Thankfully, though, I could see much better in school and on the field. Yet, down the road, they caused problems in football. I couldn't get my helmet on without the glasses being pushed down, and we didn't have goggles back then like today's athletes do. So, I only wore glasses when I played baseball.

While I was in the Pony League, it was fortunate that I had my glasses. I was the pitcher and could clearly see the catcher's mitt. Pitching was my forte, although my dad wouldn't let me throw curve balls because of the likelihood of injury. Even so, I could throw a decent curve ball. Mostly, I used change-up pitches. My fastballs weren't overwhelming, but my knuckleballs did the job. I had good control, and in one game, I threw a no-hitter! What a day that was!

Randy and I pursued baseball outside the games, often holding home run derbies. If I hit four homers, he'd have to hit five, or we didn't go home. It could take hours until we met those goals! We were very competitive, but it made each of us better. Looking back on it now, all that competition made me more confident and improved my self-esteem. Those aspects were important to me when times got tough. Sports can bring out that competitive side, and nurtures self-reliance. It also improves determination. If there's one thing I learned, it was that a person must be determined to get anywhere. Competition taught us to persevere, no matter what.

My love for sports started with baseball, but it didn't end there. I tried out for my first football team when I was in the fourth grade—it was like the Pee Wee League, or Pop Warner. We had to supply our own shoulder pads and helmets. Learning football was great! My dad didn't play football, so I learned the rudiments by being out there with kids at practice. Football has a different level of competition; in many ways, there is more intensity to the sport. Being a very strenuous sport, football is the consummate workout, but it's also a workout for the mind. This is because the offensive and defensive set ups and plays are pure strategy. Sure, a great deal of muscle is involved, but it's very much a mental sport. You could throw in some math and physics applications too.

Anyway, I was out there one day, happy to be learning the game and working as a team despite the fact that clouds were banking up, and it was getting darker. Suddenly, I looked up and saw my dad charging across the field. He was on a mission! He had a familiar look on his face—a determined look that I knew very well. I knew it was one of *those* looks, like someone was in trouble. I regarded him curiously.

"Get in the car, Jimbo. We're leaving," he said. *Leaving?* I was baffled. Practice was still in progress and I didn't want to leave.

"Dad, we're right here in the middle of practice. What do you mean, we're leaving?"

"Yeah, get in the car. We're leaving." He was emphatic.

"Why?"

"Well, if any coach leaves his players on the field when there's thunder and lightning, you're not playing for that coach."

And that was that. My football training for that year came to an end. I didn't think of it at the time, but it was a safety issue. My dad questioned the judgment of the coach who would leave us on the field when there was lightning all around. Dad was right, of course, but at ten years old, his actions puzzled me. For a while, I was angry. Basically, Dad had said, "That's it! You're done! End of discussion." I had really wanted to be part of that team, but didn't play the rest of the season. My dad had a great point, though, and he always had the bigger picture in mind. It really had been poor judgment on the part of the coach to keep playing in that kind of weather.

Despite the danger, players are still taking the field with lightning in the area. All eleven members of an African soccer team were killed when lightning struck during their game, and at least thirty baseball players over the years have been killed by lightning. So it turns out that my dad was right. This was just one example of the fact that neither of my parents would put us in a position where we could get hurt. They were very protective, and although I may not have realized that on the football field that day, they always had my best interests in mind. Time and reflection have made me realize that, and many other things, over the years.

A favorite football memory of mine is when we went to Oklahoma for a visit and my dad got tickets to the Oklahoma-Utah State game! I will never forget it. Talk about exciting! It was the first live football game I'd ever seen and the energy and excitement in the stands was truly unbelievable!

Barry Switzer was the coach. He'd been elevated to head coach at the University of Oklahoma in 1973. His record put him near the top when it came to wins. Oklahoma won three National Championships under his guidance, and when he went on to the Dallas

Cowboys, he led them to a victory in the Super Bowl over the Pittsburgh Steelers! He was a coach's coach for sure.

The day we were at the game, Joe Washington was the running back. Joe was a two-time, First Team All-American who came in third in the Heisman Trophy voting in 1974. Joe was an electrifying runner who burned up the field. He would take the pitch from the quarterback and slash through the defensive line like a rocket, spinning and cutting while tacklers lunged towards him only to find air as he wisped by them. What a thrill to see Coach Switzer and Joe! It was a day to remember.

From that game on, football was king as far as I was concerned. I remember getting home from that game and running across my front yard with a football. I would dash and dart between leaves that had fallen on the autumn ground, simulating my best #24 moves. It was then that I made my mind up I wanted to play for

24

Oklahoma. Okay, that's a strange ambition for a Texas boy given the rabid Texan fans in my home state; nevertheless, I was behind OU then, and my loyalty is still to OU. Barry Switzer and I would meet in the years to come, something I never dreamed would happen when I was at the game that day. But more about that later.

Sunday afternoons were spent watching the Cowboys and Roger Staubach, who was their brilliant quarterback. With most of us glued to the TV or radio, the sidewalks were just about rolled up on Sundays when the Cowboys were playing. I couldn't imagine not watching their games.

Yup, football became a way of life for me; I was nutty about Oklahoma and Cowboy football. Just to let you know just how much of a fanatic I was, we used to play a lot of street football when I was a kid.

One Sunday, I was out with the boys playing some ball. The street was concrete, of course, but that didn't matter—the game was all-important. I went out for a pass and lunged for it. In retrospect, that was a bad idea. I landed on my wrist and broke it and my arm in two places. At the time, I didn't realize that I had broken the bones. I got home just in time for the start of the Cowboys game. I couldn't move my right arm; it didn't matter. I was in excruciating pain; it didn't matter. I wasn't going to the emergency room for X-rays until the game was over. I can't tell you how badly my arm hurt! Yet, I was determined, and I made it through to the end of the game. Sure, I was in tears the whole time, but the game came first.

I finally made it to the ER, and sure enough, the arm was badly broken. They put me in a cast from my wrist clear up over my elbow. Fortunately, I didn't need surgery, but I was really tied up with the cast and I had it on for three or four months. The doctor told me I wouldn't be playing baseball in the spring. "I'll be ready for baseball," I insisted. And so, I was. Of course, after having the cast on for so long, the arm had atrophied. Nevertheless, I strapped a glove on the next spring and hit the field. I had to work at building up my strength, but that was okay because I wasn't going to let anything get in the way of my playing ball. My fierce determination about a lot of things seems to bring out the best in me. As it turns out, it is perhaps one of my best qualities. I'm not a quitter, even though circumstances have tried me severely.

I won't say it's been easy, and at times, quitting has seemed like the best option, but I never gave into it. I guess my innate determination was well-known. After I grew up, I ran into a man whose grass I used to mow as a kid. "I remember you as a kid. I never knew any kid that determined to play football for the University of Oklahoma," he told me. I was so determined that even in a sea of burnt orange shirts, I proudly wore red! Yes,

I learned to stand my ground, but talk about peer pressure! Even so, I was faithful to OU. I ate, slept, and breathed Oklahoma football. Fistfights would erupt, but I never relented. In the eighth grade, I went up to my social studies teacher and told her I was going to go to the University of Oklahoma.

"I'm even going to take Texas history when I get there," I proclaimed. My teacher laughed.

"They're not going to have any Texas history in Oklahoma," she said.

"I'm going to major in Texas history, and I'm going to play football for the University of Oklahoma!" I was completely sincere. I believed it. From that moment on, that was my goal. Why shouldn't it happen?

Goal setting was always a big strategy of mine. I'd mark off blocks of things I wanted to accomplish, and tick them off as I achieved them. I was religious about it. After I achieved certain goals, I would set new goals, loftier ones, the kind that make you stretch to get them. I kept at it.

Playing Texas football in Texas was pinnacle at that time, but I kept the faith. I set goals—attainable goals that I could eventually reach. There is no sense setting a goal if you can't make it.

My brother was a gifted athlete, especially in baseball. He was tall—6'4", and he was handsome. Naturally, the girls flocked to him. There were many things about him that made me jealous, but the girl thing *really* made me jealous! He also had the gift of gab and could talk his way out of anything. Robbie seemed to have it all. He ended up looking like Tom Selleck and he had that air about him. Lots of guys would have given a lot to have those attributes, me included. Consequently, he and I would get into arguments that eventually led to fights. We got into some pretty good scrapes as a result. I always thought I was right about things, even during a heated argument, and he probably thought the same thing. Over the years, I wondered if my brother ever really liked me … Perhaps it was natural to think that. Still, there were times that he was always there for me, always watching my back, always protecting me like a big brother. Go figure!

Trouble would show up and leave like a quick summer storm and then it would be all Texas sunshine where Robbie was concerned. At times, it was difficult when I'd meet former teachers who also happened to have had Robbie in their class. Without fail, most of them would ask, "How is Robbie?" It didn't matter that Robbie often skipped school. He was just a charming guy, and people gravitated to him. He also made a lasting impression on them. He found success in the computer field. To this day, I don't think he knows how jealous I was of him.

It's funny how we are, how we think and act. We can be petty and have jealousies due to our insecurities. They can wreak havoc within, particularly if you don't recognize the cause and stop them before they grow. I'll explain more about this further on in the book.

CHAPTER 3

We all have major influences in our lives, and as such, we all have special stories that we recall from time to time. Those influences and experiences help to mold us and to solidify our foundation as human. Of course, not all influences are the best. The same holds true for memories. Everyone has some things in their lives they'd like to forget. I have them, but I also have some special memories I want to keep.

I have cherished memories of my grandparents in Oklahoma and the time we got to spend there with them. After baseball season was over, we'd head up to my grandparents' farm. No matter what time of year it was, it was a great place to hang out. Summers were particularly special. Normally, I'd visit in time to help with the haying, when it took lots of hands to bring the hay crop in. My grandparents grew alfalfa and Sudan grass for the cattle. Unlike Texas, where grass grows for ten or eleven months out of the year, stores of feed were needed in Oklahoma, where it can get cold over the winter months.

I was a big kid for my age and could handle a lot of things. When I was nine or ten, I was able to help with the chores and I'd spend a couple of weeks haying at the farm each summer. Of course, my brother and sister would be there to help too. All the grandkids would rotate out during the summers to pitch in and help bale the hay. If the spring rains lagged into early summer, we could get three cuttings of alfalfa per year. If we timed our visits just right, I would get to visit with my cousins. Sometimes, if yields were high, it would take everyone working together to get bales out of the field and into the barn. We were all city kids, but it was a magical time for us. It was hard work, but I enjoyed it immensely.

Bless my grandmother's heart, she was out there doing the same work as all the men. She'd start the day by getting up early and fixing a big breakfast for us, with my little sister in tow. Around 1:00 p.m., my grandmother made sure we had a large, scrumptious supper. After we ate, we'd head back out to the fields until just before sunset and my grandmother was right there with us. She was an amazing person—to this day, she's one of the hardest working people I've ever met.

The son of a Swedish immigrant, my grandfather was also a major influence in my life. He was born in Indian Territory in 1902, and his father died when he was just two years old. He left home when he was twelve years old to get away from an abusive stepfather. My grandfather was a kind, fair, and honest man who taught me to be considerate to other people. He was big on respecting people and he taught me to do the same.

Once, while driving into town from the farm, he and I passed a man who was hitchhiking. The stranger had long hair and scruffy beard; basically, we would have described him as a hippie back in the early 1970s. My Grandpa did not hesitate and pulled the truck over, motioning for the man to get in the back so that he could give him a lift into town. Even as a young kid, I questioned the safety of this action, but my grandpa reminded me of a time when *he* had been that man, and how he'd needed a lift many times. My grandfather showed great empathy for people, and always helped those in need. During the Great Depression and Dust Bowl era of the 1930s, he let his half-siblings live on the farm to help them out. I miss both my grandparents every day, but the values they taught me live on.

My parents also reinforced this empathetic approach. My siblings and I were all taught that if we saw someone struggling, we were to help. For instance, if we saw someone having trouble getting through a door, and I was late to respond, my dad always had something to say about that.

"Why are you standing there? You need to go up there and help!"

I have to admit, I should have jumped to it without being told, but as kids, sometimes we needed to be reminded. Expected responses were also ingrained in us.

"Yes, sir. No, sir." That was just the way we were.

I learned a lot at the farm, and in my mind, being with my grandparents and family at the farm were some of the best times in my life. Even when times got rough—and let me tell you, they got rough—I could look back at the time spent at the farm with fondness. I learned plenty of life lessons there that applied to difficult struggles.

Looking back, one of the teenage rites of passage that stand out for many of us was getting a driver's license. The goal was to pass the driver's test and then be able to drive wherever we wanted to go. Since I spent time on the farm, I was able to get a head start. When I was ten or eleven, I remember my great uncle saying something that shocked me.

"Jim, get in the car and back it up." I stood there a minute, looking around and thinking he must have meant somebody else.

"Who, me? I don't know how to drive!"

"Time you learned," he said. And so, I did.

My family was very good about teaching me the finer points of backing up a truck or car with a gearshift.

"Now, let the clutch out slowly and back up." Using the clutch is like playing the cymbals: it's not so much the *how* that counts, but the *when*.

Being at the farm had its advantages when it came to learning to drive. Kids drove around most farms at times—it was necessary to help; nobody thought much about it.

I was young at the time, but they gave me responsibility and I learned to handle it. Kids in the city don't have that advantage and really shouldn't. With all the traffic, it's far too dangerous, and besides, it's against the law to let a ten-year-old loose behind the wheel. On the farm, it was a different story. Driving that early in life gave me confidence, and I accepted the responsibility and took it seriously. I also got a feeling that my family knew I could handle it. I was happy because I got the chance to spread my wings a bit. I got quite a workout driving and I got pretty good at it.

My grandmother did not have a driver's license. "Here, you get in and drive," she would say. I'd drive between pastures and follow the big equipment in the truck with my hazards on as it was moved from one pasture to another. I'd even go out on the highway for a bit while we moved stuff. Even though I was going slowly, it was awesome, and the experience greatly improved my self-assurance. Feeling pretty good about myself at the time, my grandmother told me something that I have never forgotten. "Well, once you think you're just good enough, and there's nothing else you can learn about it, watch out! That's when it'll get you!"

She was right. That warning has held true my entire life and, in many ways, remembering her words has kept me out of trouble. I can always learn something else; I don't know it all. As kids, and especially teenagers eager to cut the cord, we tend to think we know it all. But we don't. I *still* don't. That's why I keep learning. My grandmother was essentially telling me that when you get to the point of being confident, complacency sets in, and that's when you need to watch out because something will always come along to shake us up. I learned that big time. My grandmother warned me that things have a way of sneaking up on you, and boy, she was right!

I've got an impeccable memory; the times I spent at the farm seem like yesterday. All the memories are right there, front and center, and I'm glad. I also remember growing up. As I mentioned, my brother and I were both big kids, very tall. We'd come home from school and have two frozen pizzas, and then we'd still have dinner a little later. And we were still hungry—we were always hungry. Since we were so skinny, spending all our energy on growing tall, one neighbor seemed to think my dad wasn't feeding us. From the outside, it looked like we weren't getting enough to eat.

"I swear I'm feeding them," he told the neighbor. And he and our mom did. It's just that we didn't put on the weight; we only grew in height. It must have been very hard for my parents who had the constant task of trying to feed us. With voracious appetites, and continuing to grow, we had a definite need for food.

Back in the day, one of my favorite places to eat was a Mexican "All You Can Eat" buffet. It was cheap and good, and there was no way to leave the place hungry. The restaurant had small flags placed at each booth that you would raise when ordering refills of food, and my brother and I would sit at a separate booth from my parents and sister. We would promptly finish one plate, and raise the flag. After this went on several times, the manager walked by and took our flag off the table. We asked respectfully, *What gives?* He responded that his restaurant was losing money on us and that the buffet was closing. I still get a chuckle thinking about that guy — as growing boys with huge appetites, we weren't exactly budget conscious.

* * *

It's funny how things come back to us from time to time about our childhood. I was talking to my dad not long ago about an incident that happened when I was a kid. We were playing baseball in a neighbor's backyard, nearby their lamppost. You know the kind: it was like a carriage light, with glass sides; it ran on natural gas. Well, one kid was at bat and he took a swing and connected. He hit a foul ball that went up and smacked

41

right into the lamppost, breaking it. We took off and ran away.

A few days later, another neighbor told that neighbor, "Hey, those kids were playing in the backyard the other day and they broke the glass out." Mr. Fulbright, the owner of the lamppost, approached my dad and said something to him. My dad called me out of my bedroom, and I had to go talk with them. I got that feeling in my stomach; you know the type—the kind of feeling you'd prefer to do without because it's something that gnaws at you.

"Jim, I want to ask you a question … Mr. Fulbright said y'all were playing in his backyard and y'all broke the glass out of the deal. Did you do that?" my dad asked. The question was point blank.

"No, I didn't do it. Another kid did, but I was there," I answered.

"Well, you're gonna mow Mr. Fulbright's yard this summer to pay off getting that glass replaced."

"But it wasn't me ... It was another kid that did it."

"It doesn't matter. You were there, and you didn't say anything about it. You're going to go over there and take care of this man's yard to pay that off."

I was angry; it seemed unfair to me. After I got over being angry, I realized it was one of those tough lessons: even if you don't do something wrong, you must do the right thing, and mowing Mr. Fulbright's yard was the right thing to do. That lesson stuck with me—I should have said something. Letting things go only makes them worse. My dad told me it didn't matter who broke it; I still had to do the right thing. I had to apologize and step up. I had to be a man about it. No matter what excuse I had, my dad wouldn't accept it. To him, there was no excuse. It's hard for a kid receiving punishment to see things clearly. However, time has a way of giving you the proper perspective when it comes to lessons learned. My dad did the right thing in calling me on it, and taking care of Mr. Fulbright's yard was the right thing for me to do in return.

Hard lessons sting, and can be tough, yet, looking back on it all, it seems to me it was the best thing that could've happened. I learned so much from that summer-long lesson. Life is funny that way. I don't think I would have changed the situation. So, I did my time.

In dealing with any family dynamic, you find yourself in great times, and then there are times when things are not as great. Arguments can occur and words can fly—some sharp and cutting, some consoling. It's life … We all go through it. It's just that sometimes, it's hard to see things clearly during conflict, and although conflict is a sign that people care, it can often lead to disagreements. However, being passive and not interacting when you feel strongly about something isn't a good prescription for life, so we roll with the punches. Being grateful for both good times and bad helps us to be better people.

You've probably heard the old adage, "Before you judge a man, walk a mile in his shoes." That's great advice, and something that I've always taken very seriously. We don't know what sorts of burdens another person has unless we actually do walk a mile in their shoes. If we don't walk in their shoes, we couldn't possibly understand or appreciate the struggles they face. That's the lesson my grandpa showed me, and it resonated at a tender age.

The opportunity to walk in someone else's shoes can change everything about how we view the world and the people around us. I've always been empathetic with people, and after a major event in my life, that became even truer. People are awfully quick to give advice to someone who is battling an issue or situation. The fact is that we have no clue about what the other person experiences, and that holds true among family members as well.

We can also take people for granted, or just slough off things about them, not really understanding what makes them tick. Take my dad, for instance. As I said, we were very close; we still are. Still, when I was thirteen or fourteen, I couldn't figure out some things about my dad. We had a lake cabin that we would go to on weekends. My dad would ask my brother and me to go with him to help around the home, fixing it up. Robbie had his own things to do—not always, but he was often too busy. So, I was volunteered to go and help with the promise that Dad would let me drive home— it was like bribery. Dad would also promise that we could go water skiing after we finished work. Well, he had me at being able to drive home. I was at the age when driving meant everything to me, so I jumped at the chance and went with him. I think this was right around 1977 until 1979, or so.

In January of 1977, Jimmy Carter took office, and one day later, he pardoned those who had evaded the Vietnam draft. It was an act meant to heal the nation. Vets at that time were held in contempt by many people in our country, and were often spat upon when they returned. Our nation had growing pains over that war. Given that both my dad and I shared an interest in history, we would discuss these events while working on the lake house. He really did not talk about the horrors of that war, only about the places he had been around the world. Some things are best left unsaid, I guess. Anyway, my dad and I would be at the lake house, working on a deck, or remodeling rooms. My dad would be measuring and cutting boards with a vengeance. He was driven, or maybe even obsessed with being there and doing the work. I was there to help hold boards, hammer nails, and pitch in where needed.

Maybe it was the stress of raising a family at that time, or memories of the past we would rather forget, but it took me a long time to realize that working on the cabin was more than just about remodeling a few things. In fact, Dad used the time at the lake house to unwind, to get away from things, and to just enjoy himself—it was therapy for the soul, and the catharsis was good for him. Apart from working so hard, I enjoyed that time with him. It was just us, with no competition for his attention. I could share his vision of what the cabin could become after we finished the project, along with the planning and details that had to be completed. I learned about the perseverance needed to stick with a job until the last board was nailed. Although I might have resisted going sometimes, I'm glad I went. Much like the time I spent on the farm, this time with my dad helped me prepare for what was to come. Dad and I grew much closer during that special time.

I was close to my mom as well, and valued her input; however, that wasn't always the case. After my first attempt to play football bombed like a thunder clash, I desperately wanted to play football, but of course, I needed to get permission from my parents. My mother was less than thrilled about me playing football, telling me that I could get hurt. Well, I guess moms have to say that; they can feel differently than dads when it comes to football. I got that, but I insisted. Then, she brought up my broken arm. Okay, it had indeed been a bad break, but I'd gotten through it and was fine. Mom and I continued to butt heads; back and forth we went. I know she only wanted what was best for me, and I loved her for that. But how could I play for Oklahoma if I didn't get involved in football? My dream was ready to crash and burn!

My mom and I had a special bond because Dad was gone a lot for his job. She was my mentor, and guided me along the way. When I think of the torment my brother and I put her through when Dad was gone ... Sure, it was kid stuff, but I regret it. When I was younger, I remember my mom had to go to the hospital for a couple of weeks. Her mom, my grandmother, came from Kentucky to stay with us. She had come several times, but this was my first memory of her. Anyway, my mother needed surgery and would not be able to take care of us for a while. As she drove away, I ran after the car. I ran for two or three blocks, crying the whole way. I didn't want her to leave, and even though Grandma was more than capable of taking care of us, she wasn't Mom. I was heartbroken.

As I got older, I didn't want to be heartbroken again, especially when it came to something as important as playing football! I didn't relent though, and my mom finally caved. I won't say she didn't worry about me—I know that she did, but she knew it was something I had to do. She was always there for me. I didn't know it at the time, but I was about to learn that. Things were about to change in my life—in all our lives. Nothing would be the same … Nothing.

CHAPTER 4

When I was fourteen, my parents sold the house in which I grew up. Our new house was being built at the same time, but it would take nearly three months to be finished. Since we had to move ahead of schedule, my parents rented a house. After that would come the move to the new place. We had boxes everywhere; it was a mess. We all pitched in and carried the boxes into the house. My dad, Robbie, and I helped to move the heavy stuff like the washer/dryer, refrigerator, etc. Unfortunately, the temperature was extremely warm for April—about ninety degrees—awfully hot, even for Texas. Temperature records were broken, and as I recall, the whole of 1980 was off the charts. I turned fifteen just before the move.

Of course, it was chaos at the new place. We had to sleep on the floor the first night, and nobody really knew where things were. The sea of boxes overwhelmed us. We pulled items we needed each day out of boxes; we made do. Moving is never easy, and this move was just one of those things. This was the second time in six months that we had relocated, and even though we only had to move down the block, it was still a formidable task.

Since being tall and skinny wasn't the best condition for the start of football in the fall, I made plans that spring to improve my muscle mass. I added more protein to my diet, and it worked—I gained fifty to sixty pounds in six to eight months. The protein mix was nasty-tasting on its own, so I would mix it with a big glass of chocolate milk. The mix was named MLO but I affectionately called the drink "Mud, Luggie, Ouggy," which is about what it tasted like.

With the University of Oklahoma and its football team at the forefront of my thoughts, I set a goal for the summer that I would work out in the school weight room to build strength and improve my overall condition. School was about two and half miles away, and I intended to jog there. I can be very disciplined, and when I set my mind on something, I do it. At that time, being in the best physical shape was a very important goal for me.

I had to make a choice as to which sport I wanted to play in the most, so I had pulled out of basketball early in order to participate in spring football practice. Basketball had put me behind in my plans, and I was ready to leave it behind. I was getting settled into my new room, and even though it had not been quite a week since we'd moved, things were starting to feel like home. Mind you, there were still boxes everywhere and it was a time to just chill. I remember the night before that first spring practice. A Henry Fonda movie was on

TV, a film about the Miranda rights. That might seem like an odd choice for a fifteen-year-old, but I was interested in history, just like my dad. The movie was great, and I learned a lot from it. At that time, I was thinking about becoming a lawyer, and the movie involved a celebrated court case. It's funny how inspiring films can be. The movie was thought-provoking, and the idea of becoming a lawyer really appealed to me. The next day I headed for school, not realizing what was dead ahead. Football practice was scheduled for right after school. As a freshman, lots of other guys were there vying for spots and I didn't want to get lost in the crowd, and be overlooked by the coach. My only thought was, *How can I get to OU?* So many of us were competing to be on the junior varsity team; it was a big deal—at least, that's what I thought at the time.

The day was another scorcher and the field seemed incredibly hot. It was one of those steamy days where you see heat waves wafting from the street. Sweat was dripping off my forehead and the faint taste of salt was on my lips from the hydration break we'd come off a little earlier. Given the amount of water we were consuming and sweating off, salt tables had also been made available.

There we were, in the heat with pads and helmets on, but I was ready. The coaches put together what I call a skeleton defense, just so the offense could run plays against us. Some of the guys were just hanging around, sitting on their helmets. When the coach yelled out, "I need someone to play strong safety!" I jumped at the chance. My helmet was on and I sprinted onto the field, eager to prove myself. It didn't matter which defensive or offensive position I was given: all I cared about was getting in there and playing. My goal was to get noticed in a sea of kids and show that I could play ball—that was what it was all about.

The offense broke the huddle and lined up over the ball to run its play. I could see the quarterback was really looking to his right. That was my cue … It was going to be a run play. As a strong safety, I had to run support. Sure enough, the quarterback took the snap, turned to his right, and handed the ball to the running back. I charged up from my safety position and dove at who I thought was the ball carrier; another guy on defense came at the runner from the opposite direction. We both dove in for the tackle, fast, with both of us sliding off our target. It all happened so quickly and my memory of it is not so sharp. We collided, helmet to helmet, the violent impact making a thundering *CRACK*!

After that, everything moved in slow motion—it was as if time itself paused for a split second. The impact was so strong that I got knocked back. I waited to hit the ground. I kept waiting, but I felt nothing. Then, I realized I was already on the ground, on my back. My body was kind of numb and tingling. My neck was stinging like I had been stung by a swarm of yellowjackets. I didn't think much of it; I thought I'd shake it off. I fully expected to get up and be ready for another play. But that didn't happen.

My teammates ran over and offered me their hands so I could get up. I couldn't move my arms. Fortunately, before anyone pulled me up, our trainer, Doc, who was on the field at the time, saw what had happened. He ran over to me, yelling as he went for people not to touch me. You could have heard him downtown! He made sure that my neck and head were stable. I was still in my helmet, and although it was broiling hot out, I don't recall feeling the heat.

Doc was very comforting to me, but the whole time I was thinking about how weird I felt. I could talk fine and was coherent; however, my body was numb and tingling. It never occurred to me at that time that anything serious had happened—all I knew was that I couldn't move my arms or legs. It was the strangest thing because I was breathing fine. Do you know what it's like when you hit your elbow and your arm gets tingly? That's what I was feeling all over my body. Just like when I'd hit my elbow many times before, I thought the strange feeling would pass in a few minutes.

I heard Doc tell one of the guys to run to the training room and call an ambulance. I still didn't think it was a big deal. I even thought that the trip to the hospital might be unnecessary because I was sure the numbness would go away. Besides, I wasn't overly fond of hospitals. I'd gone there for my broken arm and to have my tonsils out, but other than that, I was blissfully unfamiliar with the hospital setting. I also hated needles, and never wanted to entertain the thought of getting poked with one. Anyway, all the fuss seemed overblown. I was going to be fine. I had to be. I had to play Oklahoma football.

While we waited for the ambulance, I kept telling them to put my legs down because they felt like they were bent, pulled up. They told me my legs were down. Yet the sensation of them being up was unmistakable, so I didn't understand the feeling. I thought that my legs were probably bent when I went in for the tackle, and that must have been the position they were in when the collision occurred.

We continued to wait for the ambulance. I told Doc that my dad was out in the parking lot and I asked if someone would go get him. Since the field house building was between us and the parking lot, we couldn't see the lot from where we were on the field. I insisted that my dad would be there. I just knew it was important. My dad had been there watching the practice, but I didn't think he'd seen what happened.

Doc ran someone over there to get my dad. When he hit the field, the coaches and Doc ran over to him to tell him what had happened, and he pushed through and got to me. He told me I was going to be all right, saying that the ambulance would take me to the hospital and I would get checked out. Dad always had a calming effect on me and I was thankful he was there. *What could go wrong with him watching over me?* Dad was calm and in control, although he probably didn't know the extent of my injuries. I still didn't believe that my injury was that serious. It would just take a bit of time, and I'd be back at it.

They got me into the ambulance with my helmet and pads still on. As this was before the days of tying your head down on a board, I was on the stretcher and one of the paramedics simply held my head still. My dad left his car at the school and got in the ambulance with us, and we drove very slowly to the hospital. I thought about it being Friday night. I didn't have a date, but my family usually went out to eat on Fridays. I was looking forward to it and hoped I wouldn't miss out on supper. It was already close to six o'clock.

My dad seemed uncharacteristically quiet and was obviously concerned. As I had done so many times in those stressful situations, I cracked jokes as we went, perhaps to relieve the tension. The paramedics laughed with me and we kidded back and forth. They got me to the emergency room and rushed me in. I was told they were going to try to take my helmet off so that they could take x-rays. My neck was stinging badly at this point so the thought of them taking my helmet off was disconcerting, to say the least.

They got the helmet off, but what an excruciating experience! I wasn't given anything for the pain, which was well over fifteen on a scale of one to ten. Not even my badly broken arm had hurt that much. To make matters worse, it was hard to tell what the people around me were doing. Occasionally, someone would reach over my chest and I would catch a glimpse of them. It was difficult to make sense of it all.

I thought about my injury. In the past, I'd had my bell rung a couple of times playing football; I'd seen stars, like in the cartoons. I might even have heard birds chirping. We played in a time when concussion awareness was not at the forefront of the football mindset. Also, the helmets weren't the best— barely adequate, really—but we didn't think about that stuff back then. Just like having my bell rung before, I thought it would be OK. I'd go to the sidelines and sit out a few plays, maybe a series of them, and then I'd be back in the game. However, this bell had rung out a mighty toll, and I thought I might have to sit out the spring games.

Obviously, the extent of my injuries hadn't really sunk in. At worst, I thought I had a concussion. Heck, the impact had been ferocious, but you get up and get back in the game. I was ready to get up, but there was that troubling numbness. The other player with whom I'd collided was a linebacker, a stocky kid, shorter than me. He was built like a tank. When we hit helmet to helmet, it was like being hit by a tank, or a large wave at the beach. I didn't really feel it, but I did realize that a powerful force had knocked me for a loop. As powerful as it was, I don't think I fully appreciated the true magnitude of the hit. Heck, I didn't feel a thing!

The doctors had left the room, at least that's what I thought. All I could do was stare straight up at the ceiling into the bright fluorescent lights. They were all gone for a few minutes and then Dad came in, still calm. He told me that they were going to have to take me to a hospital in downtown Dallas. Things were getting more complicated. At first, I didn't think much of it; I was still in shock. "I think this will wear off soon," I told him.

They loaded me up in another ambulance at the height of rush hour and off we went to slowly make our way to downtown Dallas. My fear of needles closed in on me. I had been in hospital for a tonsillectomy, but that wasn't anything big. This injury might be worse, but I didn't know, and I really didn't want to speculate. The long ride seemed endless. Every bump in the road and every seam in the concrete jostled me, and the pain was excruciating.

When I got to the hospital, I still couldn't move. They cut my shoulder pads off and shimmied them out from under me. They didn't dare turn me or move me. Still, I persisted in my belief that I would be okay. I had to be. I had just turned fifteen and my whole life was ahead of me. I fully expected to walk out of the hospital after getting checked over and that would be that. I anticipated a brief recovery period, but everything would be fine.

Next, they got my underwear and jockstrap off. It was an embarrassing time for me! There I was, stretched out and buck naked. A vulnerability came over me that I had never felt before. I could still only see the ceiling and only had glimpses of people moving by in my peripheral vision. I wondered what was going to happen next. I couldn't see my feet; I couldn't move my head or neck. There I was, in a world of hurt that had also allowed some confusion to seep in. It was like losing my way. True north escaped me—it was like turning around and finding myself in a foreign world. I wanted out of there.

When your world is rocked, it's disorienting. Only a couple of hours before, I had been laughing with the guys, excited to be playing ball. Life was good. Life was predictable. I'd felt in control of my destiny. Lying there now, I was painfully aware that I was no longer in control of my body. I was told they were going to put a catheter in me, but I really didn't know what it was. The medical world made me feel like an alien in my own skin. It was a perplexing time, a scary time. I wanted to go home. After all, it was Friday night! I wanted to go out and eat with my family and it was now well past dinner time. I still couldn't move. One of the nurses—I think it was a nurse ... I couldn't see—put my arms across my chest. I felt like a wire doll, or action figure that could be positioned in a certain way. But I was no action figure.

A doctor came in along with several other people who were unfamiliar to me. They must have been interns. They walked around and the doctor examined me. I really couldn't tell what they were doing. With barely a glimpse at them, I had no idea, which only added to my fear. Still, my certainty that this was only a temporary thing was firmly entrenched. I knew I would get out of there, and be fine. It might take a bit longer than expected, but I would make it. However, what happened next forced me to change my thinking.

CHAPTER 5

L ying on the gurney, now very fearful of what was going on, I heard the doctor say, "This is a bad sign." *What* was a bad sign? He was obviously examining me, but I couldn't tell what he was doing and I couldn't feel anything. His voice was somber, clinical, and rather eerie. I guess he was telling the interns what he'd found, or didn't find.

"This is a bad sign," he said again.

My optimism for walking out of the hospital anytime soon evaporated. I couldn't see the man, just the ceiling and whatever I could catch in my peripheral vision. It was like a bizarre nightmare that you hope and pray will end. I hoped I could awake and find myself at home in bed. Unfortunately, the nightmare wasn't over yet. In fact, it had just begun. The thing that made it more disturbing was that I had no control over my body. I could barely move my head and was still having trouble with my arms. I felt that my head was cut off from the rest of me. The doctor walked around, still examining me. I still felt that, eventually, I would walk out of there.

"This is a very bad sign," the doctor said again, his voice breaking into my thoughts.

I felt like a truck had hit me. Those words were sharp, harsh, and upon retrospect, even brutal. The seriousness of my situation was laid out for me. *This is really serious*, I said to myself. Suddenly, I had to reevaluate my position. It had never occurred to me until that moment that I was in serious trouble. I'd recovered from many injuries … The reality of not being able to get up and walk away this time hit me hard.

Talk about feeling vulnerable! I don't think I had ever felt that vulnerable before. Lying there, naked, and having the doctors examine me, vulnerability overwhelmed me. In the past, I'd felt somewhat in control of life's circumstances. This, however, was total chaos, and out of my control. In a way, my life and my recovery had been placed in the doctors' hands. I couldn't help myself: all the positive thinking in the world wasn't going to change my condition. I felt embarrassed, and ashamed. It's funny how emotions show up ... Sometimes they collide with one another, veering out of control and sending us on a dark, frightful journey. Things were starting to sink in. I may not have been able to feel much, but the mental pain in that moment was profound, palpable, and totally frightening. With all these strangers coming in to examine me, I felt like I was in a petri dish—an experiment for doctors who treated me like I wasn't there.

"I hope this kid makes it the next two or three days," one of the doctors said. *Two or three days?* I had no idea I was in danger of dying! My entire being revolted at the idea. The doctor was the expert and although I had beaten the odds with my badly broken arm, ultimately proving the doctor wrong, this time I had to admit I was in jeopardy. This time, I had come right up to the precipice with my numb body gripping tightly to the here and now.

The doctors were concerned about my lungs … Would they collapse? Would they do their job? If they failed, what then? I was just fifteen years old—I couldn't be near death! I hadn't even gotten my driver's license yet! I still had to make it to Oklahoma University. I was indeed in serious trouble, and yes, as the doctor had said, "This is very bad." This was all so hard for me to imagine. During all the times I had been involved in crazy sports and crazy kid things, getting bumped and bruised and even suffering some broken bones, I had still been resilient. But this time was different, much different.

I hadn't seen my dad since I'd been taken downtown to the hospital. How I wished he were there. He could always settle me down and bring me peace. I think the doctors went out of the ER room to talk to my dad; decisions had to be made about my care. I didn't know it then, but I learned later that they had discussed the treatment options.

My age was a problem, I guess. I don't know if I was too young for surgery, but my age was an issue in having it done. The doctor advised against it. I had multiple fractures in my neck, and trying to fuse all the broken bones was out of the question, so there would be no surgery to fuse the bones together. Instead, they chose traction and weights to pull my neck into alignment. This would allow the fractured bones to heal without risky surgery. That was the most viable option. It sounded simple enough, but in practice, it was horrific.

I had been enduring stinging neck pain which then turned to excruciating pain. A nurse came in and did some stuff and she was followed by several people popping in and out. My case was rare and there I was: a guinea pig for science. The doctors started talking about something; I couldn't tell what, exactly. Then I discovered they were going to put something in my head. They repositioned me, getting me ready for the procedure. I thought they would surely knock me out, give me something to put me to sleep. I longed to be put under, just like when I had my tonsils taken out. First, they knock you out, and then you wake up and the whole thing's over. That wasn't going to be the case this time. Apparently, concern arose about using anesthesia, which could jeopardize my lungs. If respiration was compromised, the heart was also at risk. Knocking me out was not an option.

I was moved to a different type of gurney or stretcher called a Stryker frame. They positioned me and got me ready so they could put screws in my head. Just the thought was enough to unnerve and terrify me. Tears started rolling down my face and I was sobbing. Being awake for the ordeal was unthinkable, but the unthinkable happened. Not being able to move a muscle, not being able to turn my neck, all I could do was scream — a lot and loud. I couldn't resist. A person's first instinct is to raise his or her arms and push away anything that's a threat; I couldn't move. The procedures involved using a tong anchored into my skull. The tongs resembled a U-shape device with two needle point screws on each side. The tong was attached to a cable so weights could be added.

So, they screwed a tong in, and I screamed. The worst part was, they figured out they screwed the tong in wrong. It was crooked and they had to take it out, reposition the tongs, and start over. I screamed again. Each turn of the screw was excruciating. With each turn, I could hear my skull give way to the pressure — it was like drilling a screw into a board. The sound was horrible, but the pain was off the charts.

When that was over, I could feel tugging on my neck. There was more pain as the forty to fifty pound weights attached to my head began to tug on my neck. Talk about medieval torture! If there was ever a description of hell, that was it! The experience was hell on earth, and then some. I think I passed out at that point. I don't remember much until I was being wheeled down the hall towards a room. Every bump and crack in the floor was sheer torture. My head hurt so badly; the pain from the screws in my head was immeasurable, but they really couldn't risk giving me anything for the pain.

When pain is that extreme, there's nothing else you can think about, except maybe wishing you'd pass out or die just to get away from it. Whether they finally gave me something for the pain or not, I don't know. Mercifully, I blacked out. Awakening, I found myself in an ICU ward. By this time, it was getting late. It must have been about 10:00 p.m. My parents came in and I was relieved to see them. No one had told me what condition I was in. Finally, my parents said that the hit on the football field was worse than most had thought, and I had been hurt badly. They told me we'd work through it, and they reassured me. I must have drifted off to sleep shortly after that.

When I awoke in the morning (I think it was the next morning) I had no idea what was going on. I recalled a dream that I'd had — one I've dreamed many times since. Each time something significant happens in my life, something big, I have this dream about a tornado, and being in a house. I can hear the tornado bearing down on me, spinning out of control, much like the situation I found myself in that morning in the hospital. If you've ever been in a tornado, you know the roar that goes with it, and the random, unpredictable destruction. No matter where I've lived, I have had this recurring dream. When life seems out of control and uncertain, I have this same nightmare. It always leaves me feeling unsettled. I awoke that day with the memory of the dream, waking up to the reality that I didn't know if it was day, or night. I had no idea … I just knew I was awake. The day before hadn't been a bad dream like the tornado dream: it was real, and there I was.

My mother kept telling me I would get through this. I didn't know how, but I trusted that she was right. Having trust was difficult when even talking to people was a problem. I couldn't turn to look at them, and I could not see them unless someone bent over me so that I could see their face. It was like listening to a radio and not really being engaged in a conversation. Other times, I wished that I could not hear what was going on around me. When a guy down the hall started screaming suddenly, I could relate to him. He screamed and kept on screaming. Faced with my new reality, I teared up. It was very difficult.

Being frustrated at my inability to see what was going around me, a nurse brought me a pair of glasses that had concave mirrors on them. Then, I could see my feet. Moreover, I could see that I couldn't move them. Nevertheless, I was grateful for the glasses; they made a difference because I could finally tell what was going on around me. The next thing I recalled was a guy coming in to say that they were going to have to flip me. I was on my back, and they were going to turn me over, tongs and weights included.

"What do you mean 'flipping?'" I asked.

"You can't lie on your back too long because you'll get sores."

They were going to put something on the Stryker frame and then they were going to flip me. I was freezing at the time, really freezing. I asked why the room had to be so darn cold. Apparently, it was better for the lungs, and kept fevers down. So, they got ready to flip me. It was kind of like having a board across your body with an opening for your face. On each end, at my feet and head, were screws that anchored the stretcher. They counted down to the flip,

"one, two, three." Flipping was done manually and it took a bit of time, and with the screws and tongs in my head, plus the weights, the pain was really amplified during this process. And when it was over, I was staring at the floor. Flipping helps the lungs because they can get fluid in them. My lungs had to be suctioned out—all part of the process. At this point, I asked my mom and dad a key question.

"How long am I going to be in this thing?" Even in the back of my mind, I thought I would heal, get out of the hospital, and move on. Reality hadn't sunk in yet.

"It might be a couple of weeks," my dad said. He kept things vague. It was always, "A couple of weeks." A couple of weeks sounded hopeful.

However, the screamer in the ward started at it again. It seemed to me he would scream 24/7. I asked my dad about him; his name was Jimmy. He had broken his back in a car accident. He must have been in terrible pain and screamed bloody murder. *I could be in worse shape … I might have been in his condition*, I thought. So, given this, even a vague two weeks seemed doable. Jimmy kept screaming, and Dad said the man was having a hard time. He must have had fifteen or twenty children. They shuffled in and out of his room, trying to console him. I wondered what it was like for them to see their dad in so much pain. I also wondered how my parents were doing as they saw me in my condition.

I realized that Jimmy might have also been going through withdrawal. Patients with similar injuries to his usually needed heavy doses of narcotics, and after seven days, an addiction was almost a certainty. Jimmy definitely had lots to deal with at the time, but all that screaming was hard on me. I couldn't sleep. I couldn't get away from the noise, and that made my pain worse. If there was ever time to get unhitched from the Stryker frame, that was it.

Finally, I told a nurse I couldn't take it anymore. I was in tears. The nurse was from India, and her words have stayed with me all my life. She spoke to me in a thick Indian accent.

"Mr. James? Do you have courage? You are going to need courage to get through this."

Her voice was so soothing and comforting; she said exactly what I needed to hear at a time when I desperately needed to hear it. *Courage. I had to have courage.* I knew I had to drill down to make it through this. Somehow, her words made sense, and although I never saw her again, she and her words have stayed with me ever since. She put her hand on my face with her fingers, caressing my eyebrows, wiping tears away, and reassuring me. It was moments like that when I could see a very dim light at the end of a very long tunnel. They represented my first glimmer of compassion outside of my family, who were all part of trying to comprehend what had happened to me.

The nurse's eloquent words drew courage out of me and made me stronger, even during Jimmy's screams and my pain. Alone, scared, and left to my own thoughts, I fought demons without being able to lift a finger. When doubt crept in, I thought of the farm, football, girls— anything to keep my fear at bay. Not really knowing if it was night or daytime, time kind of passed by me like puffy clouds in the sky. It took all the courage I could garner, but I got through the next seven days. For the most part, my dad was with me during that time; my mom too. Neither one of them got much sleep.

It sank in that my sister had been stuck at home and that my brother had been forced to step up; both lives were turned upside down. The house was still full of boxes needing to be emptied, and household items that needed to be organized. Mendy did most of that while Mom and Dad were with me. Looking at the impact of my accident, it was clear that the rest of my family faced their own ordeal. They too were suffering in their own way.

My dad told me that they were making plans to have me moved to another room with a 24/7 private nurse. Although this was a necessity, the insurance company wouldn't pay for it.

Just like flipping me in the Stryker frame, my whole world, and that of my family, had been turned upside down—one, two, three.

CHAPTER 6

When you don't sleep much for days and days, your mind begins to play tricks on you. A person needs to sleep for the brain to rid itself of old cells. It's a cleansing process. Sleep deprivation messes with the mind, and the body's chemistry, and causes tremendous stress. I was sleep deprived, coupled with trying to cope with incredible pain. I was messed up for sure.

Not sleeping much, along with dozing off and on left me unsure of what was up or down once I awoke. I remember a few instances where things became difficult. One time, I had dozed off and probably slept harder than I realized. When I woke up, I noticed my parents had gone. They had kept a constant vigil for me throughout the ordeal, and it had been a relief having them there as much as they were. I was dependent on them again in a new way, in an emotional and psychological way that was foreign to me. It was like being a little boy again, like the feeling kids get when they think something's lurking under their bed at night. Having my parents around had made me feel secure.

Never in my life had I felt as vulnerable as I did the first few days following the accident—it was scary territory for me. Anyway, I woke up, startled. I must have been flipped while I slept. When I fell asleep, I was looking at the ceiling. When I awoke, I was looking at the floor. I had an absolute meltdown! I thought I was on the ceiling! I started to scream and yell, and I must have awakened the entire floor.

I was so disoriented that it was driving me crazy. My equilibrium was off, making me extremely upset; the feeling was horrible. I felt like I was floating up to the ceiling, and there was a large knot in my stomach making me sick. In essence, I thought for sure I was dying. What else could it be? I couldn't calm down, and nothing the staff did helped. They finally called my parents, telling them I was in dire straits and that they needed to come back to the hospital.

Looking back on it, perhaps I was caught between a dream and reality. I might have been in such a deep sleep that when I suddenly woke up, facing the floor instead of the ceiling, my brain couldn't understand what had happened. Too little sleep can cause all sorts of problems. No matter the cause, I screamed and hollered. Maybe Jimmy had the same problem ... I don't know. All I did know was that I was in a horrible place. My parents lived forty minutes away. Waiting for them was like spending those minutes in hell. The time dragged on. When my dad came in, he came right over to me and stood by my side.

"What's going on?" he asked.

"Dad, I'm on the ceiling and I can't get down! I feel like I'm going to fall right out of this thing and fall on the floor!"

He said very calmly, "Son, you are on the floor and you're looking down."

"I'm not! I'm on the ceiling!"

We argued back and forth for quite a while. Finally, my dad asked me if I remembered the stories he used to tell me about the time he was in the Air Force as a navigator for pilots having trouble. Then he reminded me of the time we were on a ferris wheel. I'd had that freaky feeling and I couldn't stand it. But where I was now was far worse than any ferris wheel. He told me to pick out a spot and stare at it. "It's the same feeling you get when you turn an airplane or go up and down. You get disoriented. It's easy to get disoriented and not know where you are. Just keep staring at the point and don't look at anything else." So that's exactly what I did, and little by little, things got better. I kept staring at the focal point, and the feelings subsided. My dad hung in there with me. He's a real hero! My dad knew what made me tick. I eventually calmed down thanks to my dad, and his advice.

A few days later, they decided to try me on some food. I hadn't eaten anything since I'd been admitted. The lack of sleep coupled with the lack of food was definitely a tough combination. Well, they brought me something to eat. I'm not sure what it was, but it didn't matter. I was so glad to be eating something—anything! Before long, though, I started to feel sick. I started to choke! I couldn't move my head or help myself. I was lying on my back, looking straight up when I ate, and for some reason, it made me sick. I started to vomit—a bad thing when you can't move your head and neck. I was in bad shape, and at risk of drowning in my vomit. The feeling was horrible. They used suction on me to get the vomit from my mouth and I couldn't get rid of it fast enough. The sensation of getting close to drowning was frightening. Vomit was drooling out of my mouth, and unfortunately, I aspirated some of it and it got into my lungs.

Every couple of days, the fluid would build up in my lungs and I'd start choking again. They had to use suction again, and I think they put a tube through my nose. Being completely helpless, I depended solely on the care from other people. They had a problem getting the tube up my nose, probably because my brother and I had wrestled one time, and I ended up with a broken nose and also developed a bone spur that was a barrier to the tube. Having the delay in getting the suction going was alarming. I couldn't cough, but needed to— desperately.

In the process, the bone spur was knocked out of the way and it went down my throat, causing yet another problem. It was one thing after another. The injury to my neck was bad, but the other complications made it more difficult. So many things cropped up all at once, it was like trying to survive on a battlefield: eventually, you get a little gun shy because you don't know what you're going to be hit with next. After these harrowing experiences, I soon realized that a tube can be inserted in pretty much every opening in the body.

I now had a new set of fears to battle ... I was afraid to fall asleep because I might wake up completely disoriented again, and I was concerned about eating because I didn't want to choke. Just like a baby, I had to be fed and watched over for fear something would happen, such as drowning in my own fluids. My mind wandered often to *what if...?* But I didn't want to go there. Once again, I remembered the nurse's words: "Courage. You must have courage." The problem was, I wasn't sure where to find it. Sure, it's something deep down inside of us, but at the time, I was looking at things too closely. Courage seemed elusive to me. I was put on antibiotics and eventually, things got better. Yet recent incidents were still on my mind and would come back to haunt me. I had to have my lungs suctioned four or five more times so I was put through the wringer for sure. Finally, once my lung infection had improved, and after two weeks in the ICU ward, I was moved to a private room.

My parents had secured a couple of private duty nurses who would keep close tabs on me. I still had to endure the Stryker frame and traction on my neck, but anything was better than the ICU ward. The first nurse was old school. She wore a sterile white uniform, and topped her head with a nurse's cap every day. I must admit I was a little cranky, but we butted heads from day one. She would tell me what to watch on TV, and when the lights were going off. I felt like a baby, and soon, it all came to a head. I'd had enough of poking, prodding, tubes, turning, noise, and especially a nagging ole nurse. To make matters worse, the surroundings were uninspired: blank walls, a lack of color, and the sterile environment compounded my negative feelings. I missed being at home and having my room set up the way I liked it. It's funny which comforts I missed; the lack of familiarity and sense of safety that "home" naturally brings bothered me immensely.

When my parents made it to the hospital that particular day, they could sense I was unusually upset. Parents have a way of knowing their child is hurting, and boy, was I hurting. My spirit was broken, and my will to carry on was slowly evaporating. To be perfectly honest, I was feeling sorry for myself. My dad got on the floor and looked up at me so that he could pry out what was wrong. I started to sob, my tears falling on his shirt. *I've had enough, Dad. I have no more fight.*

I was expecting a pep talk. You know, something like a coach would say when you're down by two touchdowns at halftime—the kind of speech that would lift the team from their funk and they'd go out in the second half and fight to the end—so my dad's reaction shocked me to the core. To this point in my life, I'd never seen my dad cry. His eyes filled with tears and he began to sob. My reaction was swift and almost immediate as I yelled, "STOP! Please STOP!" At that moment, I realized that I was not the only one hurt by this accident … my mom, dad, siblings, friends, and even the community were all hurting. I said, "We will get through this ordeal together, but I don't want to see you cry again, Dad." I felt ashamed and selfish. It might seem strange, but it was more painful for me to see my father crying over me than it was for me to cry for myself, which was how things had gone up to this point.

My mom and dad asked what would make things better for me. In my room at home, I had posters on the wall and I really wanted something like that in the hospital. With all the noise, it was nerve-wracking. There was nothing I could do to get away from it. It occurred to me that the place was devoid of music. Sure,

I had a television, for which I was grateful, but I missed my tunes. I wanted to hear some Willie and Merle and other singers. Music was important to me. They say that music soothes the savage beast—well, I was a teenager in a world of hurt and I really wanted my music. I asked Dad if he could find that Ray Charles album he always talked about. My mother got the word out, and a few days later, I had a brand new 8-track tape player and record player, kind of a luxury item back then. My old middle school principal took up a collection and bought it for me.

My mom put posters on the wall, and I got my tunes. Someone found that ole Ray Charles album at a garage sale and I was all set. It seems like such a small thing now, but at the time, it was huge. I really needed that sense of home. Most of us groove along to our music, either tapping our feet, dancing, or whatever. I could no longer dance and I didn't feel the music the way I used to, but I was happy to have the songs to take me away for a while.

Songs have a way of reminding us about people and places to the point that most of us can say where we were or what we were doing when a certain song is played; I was no different. It may very well have been a nostalgic journey for me listening to the tunes I loved. It was the first time I got to hear the tunes after the accident, and it meant a lot to me because for a while, I was transported to another place or time, at least in my mind. I could get lost in the groove and just block out the here and now. Looking back at that time, the music was therapeutic for me: it quieted me down, and I could drift along with it. Most kids at the time were listening to a whole different kind of music, everything from the Beatles to rock to the Eagles. However, I had developed different tastes. Music is subjective, I guess. While it can be a universal thing, ultimately it comes down to our own likes and dislikes.

I remember when I was in the car with my mom and dad, driving along. We had the radio on, and I was flipping through the stations, trying to find a good one. A Paul McCartney song came on.

"What is that stuff?" my dad asked. I don't think he was a fan. My dad was more into fifties rock, and singers like Jerry Lee Lewis and Elvis Presley. He wasn't quite up for the modern stuff. I guess every generation lays claim to their music.

My mom had chimed in, "If he wants to listen to that, it's okay."

Well, even to this day, I'll still take Willie and Merle. Anyway, being out of ICU was a big relief, but I still had a private nurse twenty-four hours per day. Considering the events that happened, it was good to have someone there, but I never really had alone time. Maybe that was a good thing … otherwise, maybe I would have thought about things too much.

Even after the accident, I tackled circumstances head on, and drove myself to make it through. Basically, I was still me, determined to make the best of things. Feeling sorry for myself would have gotten me nowhere; in fact, I think it might have made things worse. I'm not saying I never got down—I did. I'm not saying I wasn't frustrated by my new reality—I was. The thing was, I had always strived to do my best, and the recovery period for me would be no different. I was going to get through it the best way possible, and fight to make progress, no matter what. Big words and big goals, I know, but the things that come easily aren't as valuable as the things that come with difficulty. I kept telling myself that, anyway. I didn't know where I was headed; however, I wasn't going to give up. It really boiled down to taking things one day at time. Sometimes, looking ahead was reduced to one hour, or one minute, but I was going to make it—I had to.

Looking back on things, I really didn't get much of a rundown about the future, and how to handle it. There wasn't any rehab, so to speak, only minimal stuff. It could have been that I wasn't out of the woods yet. The days were spent surviving from one thing to the next, and there was always one more thing with which to cope.

At first, I really couldn't have visitors other than my parents; even Robbie and Mendy couldn't come to see me. And my grandparents had driven down from Oklahoma only to find out they could not see me either. By this time, my mother had realized that phone calls to friends or receiving cards and letters might benefit me. My grandparents had left a message for me on cassette tape, and this started a trend. My dear mother would gather up people and they would take turns at the mic, recording their messages. I heard from aunts and uncles, cousins, teachers, coaches, and school friends. I could listen to them over and over. What a difference that made! Yet, it was bitter-sweet: the situation was tough for everyone, and hearing my family's and friends' voices on tape was a moving experience.

I hit some very rough spots in the first three-week period. People had to lean over me to talk so that I could see them. I was still in the Stryker frame, and that meant I was still being flipped every few hours—it was gruesome. I reached points where it all seemed too much for me. I guess it's like people who have major surgery and they get the post-surgery blues ... People often break down and cry. I think it's the emotional upheaval, and the battle that's being waged. Eventually, we hit a tipping point, and something must give. That's the way it was for me: a giant tipping point, or more like hitting a big, emotional, brick wall. Ultimately, I felt like an overinflated tire. *Wham!* Every once in a while, I would blow out from all the pressure.

Seeing my dad break down and cry was horrible. There was so much to deal with, and no one really knew how. Accidents can be sudden and unexpected, leaving people at a loss. We aren't really trained in how to get through life-changing events—put in a position of no return, we are forced to change and to play the hand we're dealt. Things were never going to be the same for me. The present was bumpy; the future, if there was going to be one, might be even bumpier.

I had a recurring question: *What next?*

CHAPTER 7

Obviously, the stress and strain on my family from the accident was intense. We had a close family and we got along well, but we had arguments, just as most families do. The dynamics of family life are naturally in a state of flux: they ebb and flow, settling down into the predictable, and then suddenly changing. That inevitable change in tides happened before my accident, as well as after. Ours was family life as we knew it. We weren't the Cleavers, by any stretch of the imagination—we were the Wallgrens, an average American family working hard to stay together.

Within the chemistry of our dynamic family situation, I was the jokester, always wanting to execute an end around when things got too heated. I knew then (and still know now) that a little bit of humor in difficult circumstances can go a long way to ameliorating any situation. Naturally, that humor wasn't always well-received, but it did provide a light-hearted derailment during heated arguments. During the days immediately following my accident, everyone's nerves were on end. When my dad broke down, lying on the floor under the Stryker bed, I couldn't take any more, so I quipped about something, and said we'd get through it. From that moment on, the emotional tide turned and I again began to use humor to help get through things.

Humor is good for the soul, the emotions, and the body. It can have a healing effect, and at that point, my family and I needed all the healing we could get. Laughter has been known to be a wonder when it comes to healing; in fact, scientific proof exists that laughter truly is the best medicine. Laughter releases endorphins—those wondrous chemical components that make us feel better. Another by-product of laughter is the stress-reducing qualities it has. Did you know that a good belly laugh reduces stress hormones, increases immune cell count, and can act as a powerful antibiotic? A hearty laugh wards off infection and helps the body heal. I was certainly in need of all of that, and so was my family.

We were a team, and we had to stick together. If one member suffered, we all suffered: a universal fact. Working through something alone is extremely difficult, but being an athlete and appreciating the team perspective, I had come to know first-hand the advantages of teamwork. My family had a great deal to get through during that time, so I made up my mind to joke about the circumstances. What else could I do? Sure, I could feel sorry for myself, and there may have been a few times when that happened. Overall though, I kept pushing to do better, to be better, and to live.

When the accident occurred, other important things in my life were abruptly suspended. I wasn't just physically frozen, unable to move ... there was another significant change that I wasn't aware of then. I was absorbed in a battle with the moment and the injuries, but there was something else rendered immobile besides my physical body: the rest of the kids around me went on with their lives. They had their Friday night and weekend activities, and the following Monday after I got hurt they were back at school, dealing with the grind of classes and jostling to fit in socially.

My social life, however, and the circle of people around me changed dramatically. The routine of school and sports, family time, and just hanging out were all replaced by new circumstances. While my friends were at school, I was hanging out with the people in the ward, all dealing with various degrees of pain, and the severity of their injuries. Gone were the lunchroom interactions with my friends ... Instead of hearing laughter, idle chat, and jocularity, I heard screaming and crying; I participated in some of that as well. Instead of talking with girlfriends, I had to deal with nurses, some of whom, as I mentioned, were cranky. Some, like the Indian nurse, were comforting, but I had been thrown into a whole new social circle marked by many professional interactions that were somewhat sterile as medical and hospital staff did their job of taking care of me. They had to interact, but it was on such a clinical level that it was devoid of emotion. I understand that's partially the intent behind it—if medical personnel become too emotionally attached to their patients, it could be detrimental to all involved.

Yet, as a fifteen-year-old kid, it was hard to get beyond the chill of those interactions. My life had been changed in an instant. Yes, friends would call, and I would get cards, but in the big picture, I was ostracized. The lives of my friends continued unabated and I wouldn't have had it any other way; still, my life came to a standstill. Progress was slow, and I was surrounded by a social and clinical structure that was not conducive to building a normal, well-rounded life. Not only had the feeling in my hands, arms and legs been numbed, so had my interactions with other people.

My family did the utmost to help me. My parents stepped up, and if it hadn't been for my mother's phone call and letter campaign, things would have been much worse for me. I was essentially in an incubator, thrown into a gestational period where my life was being changed, and rearranged. I had no idea where I would end up, but I decided to make the best of things. Little did I know what a challenge that would be.

The whole experience was like looking out the window while the world and everyone in it zoomed by; people were busy living. While I was in the Stryker frame, it seemed to me I was frozen in time, all the while knowing that the world kept turning and that people were engaged in their lives. I now viewed and calculated the concept of time much differently. My time was broken down into the hospital routine: I woke and ate at pretty much the same time every day. Being a patient, and a captive one at that, time is segmented and often feels stalled. My mother wondered what would help me pass the time. Maybe my situation was similar to that of a prisoner ... What can pass the day away while you wait? I longed to be out of the hospital and be free. I longed to walk too, but as the days went by, it was obvious that walking wasn't going to happen. So, I was left with time—the time between the segments of the hospital routine—and I had to get through it.

The view from my Stryker frame was limited and changed 180 degrees whenever they flipped me. During the flip, I would get glimpses of things in my room. My mom got the idea of stringing cards across the room that people had sent me. It made the atmosphere less drab, and I was extremely grateful for all the cards and letters that people sent! Yet, it still wasn't home. I had some tough times, but I pushed ahead. I got to listen to my Willie Nelson tunes; he was big at the time. His outlaw music was popular, and I was a huge fan. I had an

African American private duty nurse who helped me. His name was Irv.

I asked Irv to put in another 8-track tape once an album had finished. Music poured out of my room, helping me so much by transporting my emotions to a different place. I loved it! I needed it! Irv expanded my musical appreciation with the likes of BB King, exposing me to a different world of tunes. The music permeated my mind as I drifted to the lyrics and the melodies. Taking my mind off things and allowing me to escape, music was powerful therapy for me, and for a time, the world melted away. Pain was better; I was better. In a real sense, music mentally saved my life. Sure, when the tunes stopped, I was back in the moment, tied to my surroundings, but the oasis that music provided, the sweet respite, could be summoned again by more tunes. Music can touch us so completely, transforming us. I don't know how I would have survived without it.

I was often asked during this time about my spiritual coping mechanisms, and whether I turned to my faith to get me through the hard times. Although going to church on Sunday was normal in rural Oklahoma, my family really wasn't spiritual. My dad would occasionally go with friends; however, after his Vietnam experience, something changed. I really don't know about my mom. My family just didn't have an active spiritual life. I'd asked my parents about it when I was younger: they told me that at some point in my life, I would come to my own conclusions about faith.

"We're not going to force you to go to church," my mother had said.

It was a decision I had to make; I was on my own to find out about my spirituality. I did go with friends to all kinds of different church denominations—it seemed that they found such comfort and certainty in their faith. I just found more questions than answers. Still, I was envious of them.

In the hospital, a minister would come by and we'd talk for a while. I always appreciated chatting with someone. The minister was a nice man and had lots to say, particularly about God. It was his job and he didn't miss an opportunity to talk about God, which is understandable. There were platitudes and assurances during those talks that would rub me the wrong way at times. He meant well … I never questioned that, but his persistence got to me. Finally, I told him to stop talking about it; he did. I guess my spiritual decision-making wasn't ready to meet my personal decision-making. When he visited me after that, we stuck to playing chess. I love a good game of chess and it helped my mind to stay active. I appreciated the time he spent every week visiting me. Our friendship changed, and for me, it was more comfortable.

The minister wasn't the only one to bring up God—lots of cards and letters I received had that as a continuing theme. If I prayed hard enough, God would heal me; I needed to trust in God, and He would act. On and on it went. I had this inner dialogue going on in my mind, and perhaps even in my soul, predicated on some key questions: If there was a God, how could He put me in the circumstances in which I found myself? How was it possible, if God loved us so much, that people had to go through such misery and suffering? Why did *I* have to go through this injury and the horrible results? Why would God interrupt my life with this injury? I had so many questions ... My mind raced with questions upon questions but I got no real answers. I couldn't comprehend the spiritual side of things and how God relates, or doesn't relate, to our lives.

To make it harder to cope, some of the letters I got with strong spiritual overtones stated that I would walk out of the hospital! Was it merely a matter of God? Was it a matter of belief? I don't know. In my teenage analysis of the situation, I was left with even more questions and only got the proverbial crickets chirping while waiting for answers. Often, there wouldn't even be crickets. I had ministers tell me that God had a plan for me; I don't know what that plan was. It seemed to me that if I put that plan into something like a football playbook, it would be obvious the plan wasn't working—at least, I couldn't see that it was working. There might well have been a plan, but I was clueless. I was hurting, and still I searched. I searched as hard as I could for answers.

I was at a crossroads on many levels. Which way should I turn? What should I believe or what shouldn't I believe? I was in a quandary, in a battle being swarmed by bees or wasps, only the battle was waged against the Whys! Why was I injured? Why couldn't I walk again? Why must I lead a life so foreign and painful? The Whys buzzed around me, almost disorienting me. For a while, the battle was obsessive. I fought with the Whys and even the Why Nots. Answers were elusive, and the constant roar of questions in my mind took their toll. I turned to music, and tried to focus on the songs: the lyrics about people, life, and love. When the music stopped, the Whys came back with a vengeance and they are still with me today. I try not to let them rule my life, but I'd be lying if I said I still wasn't searching for answers to the Whys and Why Nots, still searching to find the missing pieces to fill the voids in my mind and heart.

Spending a lifetime trying to get all the pieces of the puzzle to fit has been problematic. I have come to some conclusions, and one is that we don't really have control over our lives. We might think we do, but that's not the case. Obviously, there wouldn't be all the negativity and sorrow in our lives if we did have control. The fact is that misery is part of our existence. In some lives, if allowed to be, it can be a major part: circumstances do dictate how we end up. Nevertheless, we can build a rampart to keep those circumstances from devouring us. Yes, I had my humor, I had my life, and I had the choice whether or not to keep pushing to make a new life for myself. I was fortunate not to have died, even though the minute by minute battles I faced after the accident were like dying mini, painful deaths. But I didn't let those battles define me, and who I was. I may not have known the Whys about the aftermath of the accident, but I understood, even at fifteen, that a person can adapt, if given half a chance—if the person *wants* to adapt.

Doing my best to overlook the chasm between my situation at the time and the far horizon of my future, I had a decision to make.

CHAPTER 8

My mother continued to read 'Get Well' cards and letters to me as they came in; it helped. One day, she read a card from a kid with whom I'd gone to school. Meeting in middle school, and then going on to high school together, we'd known each for quite a while. We had both ended up on the football team. He mentioned in the card that he hoped I was feeling better, and hoped I would get well soon. He also stated that everyone was pulling for me. Those are great sentiments and nice to hear. It's nice to know that people care. At the time, I admit I might have been a bit cynical when I was having a bad day. Nevertheless, the thoughts behind those wonderful cards helped me tremendously.

Then, my friend wrote something that threw me for a loop. It was like getting tackled, blindsided out of the blue ... *Wham!* The guy wrote that he hoped I would get better and walk out of there because he didn't know if he could handle seeing me in a wheelchair.

There it was! A humongous dose of reality as potent as anything the doctors could prescribe, guaranteed to upset your stomach and leave you with that strange feeling near the solar plexus. *A wheelchair?* Oddly enough, I hadn't looked too far into the future. I was still eking towards it, not paying too much attention. I was focused on getting through the day. Now, there was no escaping it: I had to confront the fact that I would spend my life in a wheelchair.

Wheelchairs are game changers in many ways. For people walking down the street, a person in a wheelchair can be a problem. Excluding the fact that people might need to walk around, or step aside to allow the person to get by them, there's the awkward moment to deal with—whether you're the person walking, or the person in the wheelchair.

People engage in this inner dialogue as they near a person with a disability; an inner debate ensues. *Do I make eye contact? Do I say anything?* Perhaps it stems from the fear that something horrible might happen to them, and they too might find themselves in a chair. Perhaps it's feelings of guilt that they are able to walk. Whatever it is, there are uncomfortable moments when the disabled and the healthy meet. I'd been there a time or two myself, but really hadn't given it much thought. Now, I was forced to think about it. Up until the moment that my mother read that card to me, I can honestly say that a wheelchair hadn't been on my radar, not at all.

A lack of communication was the norm. No one on the hospital staff had come in and said, "Look, Jimbo, you're not going to get around, and you better get used to the idea that you're going to need a wheelchair."

People walked on eggshells in terms of what was said. With that message in the card, a trumpet blast sounded in my head. A wheelchair was going to be part of my life; I would be tethered to it. If I wanted to get anywhere, I'd need to use it.

How would people deal with me? Would my friends still be friends if I showed up at school in a wheelchair? I had a great deal to think about. A wheelchair had such negative connotations, permanent connotations from which there would be no half-time, no bye week, and no off-season. It would be the new order of the day. It would certainly become an extension of me.

I wasn't ready to go there, not yet, but I had to. After the other shoe dropped, I had to consider what was going to happen. How would I relate to my friends? A sentence to life in a wheelchair had a lot of drawbacks. Sure, you could get around in a chair and that helped, but often, it's difficult for those in wheelchairs to access certain buildings and other areas. And forget about stairs! Forget about a lot of things.

I realized I needed to spend some serious time thinking about the logistics and the ramifications. I needed to think about the "new" me. The social aspects also figured into the mix. What about girls? What about dating? Would any girl want to date a guy in a wheelchair?

Talk about feeling like a hedgehog! Emotionally, I curled up a bit and needed to regroup. Always able to work through situations and tackle the hardest tasks, I discounted my resilience when I first contemplated life in the chair.

No, it wasn't the electric chair—there were worse things. Yet, it was alien to my psyche, to my perception of myself. I would be forever linked to the chair. I would no longer be simply Jimbo Wallgren, but Jimbo Wallgren in the wheelchair. The wheelchair and I would be inextricably linked until a miracle, or some surgical intervention took place, or I died.

At fifteen, life now seemed arduous, long, and uninviting. Sexual exploration would no longer be possible. *Would it?* And oh, how the chair would change the dating scene! I hadn't even gotten my driver's license yet. I supposed that in my normal, self-assured moments before the accident, had I been thinking clearly and not in pain, it would have been normal for me to figure out how to pop wheelies in the chair.

Nothing looked promising after that card, and it would take a bit of doing to get my old self back again. Too many variables had been thrown at me all at once. More What Ifs and more doubts accumulated like heavy snow. My mind and heart were weighted down. All the expectations of a fifteen-year-old were blown up that day—*blam!* I hadn't even given any thought as to how I was going to get into my house! How was I going to get to the bathroom? The obstacles in my path seemed especially insurmountable at that moment.

Then I got hit with something bigger than the sentiments in that card. Something hit me even harder, right between the eyes … Fear! That's what it was: fear, a cold and palpable fear, visceral and menacing. I seldom, if ever, was afraid, but this time it pounced on me, enveloped and captured me. It was gruesome; it was very real. I didn't like how it made me feel. They say that fear is the great leveler, and so it was for me. I was leveled all right, plain and simple.

Strange what some words in a card can do! My parents kept reassuring me, supporting me— they said it would all work out. My dad had a peaceful presence, and he was a leader. People believed what he said. I believed him; it would somehow all work out.

However, that didn't stop the doubts. They were there, and at times, they were a heavy burden. I heard many platitudes in one form or another those first weeks after the accident. A disparity existed though between the platitudes and the reality of it all. The reality of the wheelchair and the Do's and Don'ts that went with it messed with my mind. Doubts can be like weeds that winnow their way into your mind and heart. By their gnarly nature, they wrap themselves around the reassurances you've been given, and before long, those reassuring words are choked out, leaving a more powerful doubt behind.

Like a multi-level chess game, I knew I had many battles to fight, and while I got better at playing chess, the doubts had me on the run. It's funny ... The music in my room brought many visits from the hospital staff, who would hear the music and stop by. We'd chat about little things, about music, and they would go on about their day. It was about this time that the expense of the private duty nurse was hitting home. Dad didn't complain, and he was there every day to see me. No matter what, he made it a point to be there. How I needed him to be there for me! I didn't need to ask. He was just there. But it must have been tough for him with the responsibilities he had at his new job. Both my dad and mom had a great deal to handle, more than I could imagine.

My dad's job was working for a milling company in Denton. They milled corn and flour into pre-mixed products like biscuits and cornbread. He was a salesman there. All his natural talents and abilities helped him in sales. There was just a good sense about him, underscored by leading a good example, and I'm sure that's why he did so well. The owner completely understood what my dad was trying to handle and told him to take whatever time he needed to be with me, and to take care of things outside of work. I'm glad my dad had an employer like that, especially at that time. The stress of it all made things doubly hard. But as he would say, it would all work out. I had to keep telling myself that, and maybe my dad also had to convince himself that everything would be okay.

This was also the time that the insurance company reared its head and started backpedaling. It put my dad in a bad spot, and things got heated with the insurance carrier. The owner of the company that my dad worked for told the carrier to step up and cover more. He even threatened to pull the insurance for his entire company if they didn't comply. When anyone buys insurance, they think they're covered, but it's really only when accidents or illness happen that we discover what is truly in our policies. Fighting an insurance company is never easy, and my dad must have felt like he was on the ropes more than once. After all, he was taking on a Goliath. Still, he kept on swinging and fighting for what he believed was right.

Meanwhile, my parents' savings were on Code Blue. The hospital expenses, even with insurance and especially with the private nurse, ate away at their funds to the point that they were skating on financial thin ice. Fortunately, family, friends, and people in the community realized the inordinate burden my parents carried and they stepped up. They organized many benefits in my name: "Swim for Jim" and "Jimbo's Jamboree" to name a couple. People donated generously, and helped to defray costs.

It's times like these that people's true natures are exposed. We were blessed to have so many people come to the rescue and help us to make ends meet. When something happens to us as individuals, it's hard not to feel guilty when the rest of the family is put to the test. Although my injury was an accident, I still had twinges about causing financial strain on my family, a stress that was also transferred to my brother and sister. With Mom and Dad struggling to make ends meet, I'm sure they felt that they weren't getting the usual amount of attention.

The benefits and fundraisers helped all of us, and I was humbled by the generosity of people, many of whom were total strangers. When communities come together like that to help a family in need, it restores faith in one's fellow man. My gratitude for the compassion and empathy shown to my family cannot be expressed in words. "Thank you" doesn't seem like quite enough, but even today, I still try to express my thanks for the support we received.

My hometown of Garland also stepped up and got behind me. We had three or four high schools there and I'd get letters from people who went to other schools. I even got letters from our sports team competitors. The warmth and love that was offered was overwhelming, and we couldn't have made it through without the good people of Garland. My mother became the public face and voice of my plight—perhaps her TV career made her well suited for the job. She fielded countless calls, and answered letters from well-wishers. Both the local paper and *The Dallas Morning News* had stories about me. Not only did the articles bring attention to my plight, but they also served as a wake-up call about the possible dangers associated with playing football. With all the news going out about the accident, a big benefit was planned. It was a musical revue type show called "Jimbo's Jamboree", featuring country music. The show was held at the stadium where I got hurt, with the performers standing close to where the accident occurred. Artists flocked to the event and the town heartily supported it.

Sadly, I couldn't be there to watch the show—I wasn't well enough—so I was relegated to my 8-track music. Then, Southwestern Bell found out that I wasn't going to the show. They hooked up a direct line to my hospital room so that I could listen! Through the conference line and speaker, I could hear it all. It was extremely moving. So many people came to that benefit to help me and my family! I made up my mind at that point that I was going to keep on fighting. I had to … I owed it to my family and friends, and I owed it to myself. After things settled down, some of my friends and teammates visited me at the hospital. It was great to see them. There was a twinge, though, looking at them and then watching them file out to go home. They went on with their lives while I was left behind to figure out how to get on with mine.

Something wonderful occurred after the benefit: *The Dallas Morning News* once again covered the Jamboree in their paper. It was nice of them to do, and it led to a surprise.

One day in my room, not long after the benefit, I was lying there wearing those mirror glasses. All of a sudden, I looked up and standing there was Mike Ditka! At the time, Mike was the assistant coach of the Dallas Cowboys. Mike had played originally for the Chicago Bears and was a heroic tight end, number 89, who earned the reputation of Iron Mike, no doubt about it. He was later picked up by Dallas and played tight end for the Cowboys, still sporting his legendary number 89!

Well, there he was standing in my room. He had stopped by to see how I was doing. He presented me with an autographed football signed by the entire team, and also brought a projector with him and some game films which we watched together.

It was a bittersweet experience for me. I was blessed to be in the same room with one of the greatest football players of all time, now an upcoming assistant coach. He'd taken the time to visit me, just a kid, someone he didn't know. The game films were great to watch to a point, but there was a sore spot, perhaps an even bigger spot than I realized, and that wound got some salt poured into it that day. I had a passion for football, and watching the Cowboys' game films didn't quench that, but the painful irony of the situation did bring a lump to my throat. It was because of my passion and involvement in football that I was now lying on a Stryker frame.

CHAPTER 9

Life certainly has its twists and turns. Mike Ditka wasn't the only Cowboy to stop by—other Cowboys came by to visit me as well. Surprisingly enough, the Dallas Cowboy Cheerleaders even stopped by. It was a kid's dream come true! Their visit created quite a commotion! It was great to have those people visit with me for a while. Suddenly, I was on the good side of the doctors. It's amazing what a cheerleader visit will do! It was long before social media kicked in, but it was far more effective. I'm sure the news coverage and the benefits helped to get the word out. It was fantastic for people to take time out of their day to visit a fifteen-year-old kid. Those visits gave me plenty of things to reflect on, especially when times were tough.

Football heroes weren't the only people to visit. For some reason, Ray Wiley Hubbard, the singer-songwriter from the South Dallas area, stopped in to see me, leaving a signed album. Ray's a scruffy kind of guy, who looks like he is hung over. When he visited me, he was accompanied by his beautiful girlfriend, making for quite the odd couple. His voice is unusual, his songs even more so. From "Snake Farm" to "Redneck Mother" and other notable tunes, his music is just like Ray himself: outside the box, and colored outside the lines.

Even the great Barry Switzer, the head coach of Oklahoma, sent me an autographed picture. He'd seen a picture of me with my parents and wrote that he assumed I was an Oklahoma fan from my attire. Oh, yeah! If he only knew! Coach Switzer was down in the Dallas area on a recruiting trip when he stopped by. That stung a bit. Okay, it stung a lot. In another few years, I would have been just about ready to think about moving on to Oklahoma and their football program. Of course, I still needed to put in the work and with a little luck, I might have been one of the kids he recruited. It was my goal and dream, but my dreams were tackled at the one-yard line. The end zone beckoned me, and yet, fate had stepped in. I would never reach my goal. My last tackle had been it; football and all its glory were now relegated to TV. Gone were the two-a-day practices, the pep-rallies, the Friday night games—all of it gone. Coach Switzer went on to write that if I were a Longhorn fan, I was free to put his picture on the wall and throw darts at it. Fat chance that was the case! I was a Crimson and Cream fan until the end, a bittersweet obsession. Still, I wondered ... what if?

Finally, it was time for PT (physical therapy) and OT (occupational therapy). I was still in the Stryker frame, but the therapists would do what they could to help me, for example, they'd work on my arms. It's weird to see your body moving and not be able to feel it. Part of the great feeling in sports was the workout:

the sweat, and at times, the pain and muscle aches. At the end of a practice or a game, you'd feel great—maybe worn out, but it was a super feeling. I didn't get that with the therapy. I was worn out, but missed the rush of physical exertion and how it helped me to feel better.

I was still in the heat of battle, but enclosed in a cocoon without feeling. Still in traction, and still in need of a private duty nurse, it took me some time to assimilate. The private nurses, like Irv, didn't have that much to do. They'd check on my urine output, change the tunes for me, or help me with whatever I asked. Their shifts must have felt long due to the lack of tasks. It was great that they were there though, and I did feel more secure. I still wasn't eating like I should and was so thin that it scared people. The food wasn't the greatest, so perhaps food had lost its appeal and subsequently, I lost the weight. It could also have been that practically choking on more than one occasion and nearly drowning in my own vomit helped me acquire a psychological block when it came time to eat. Call it a subconscious fear, but food was no longer an enticement—it was a necessity, and even then, I had to push myself to eat.

To help pass the time, I'd talk to Randy, Brian, and Rodney on the phone. They had lots to share about school and about football practice. That was a tough one, since I only had the day-to-day war stories to talk about. These conversations made it apparent that I was living in a medical fishbowl, where my movement was restricted. The Stryker frame was the bowl, and my view was limited to the small room. Randy and the guys were living in the ocean of life with expansive views of things not yet tried calling to them. On the other hand, I heard the calls coming over the hospital intercom for doctors and Code Blues, a music all its own, a singular rhythm, at times predictable, and often annoying.

Yet, despite those annoyances, I adapted, and the hospital became a home away from home, ever foreign, but at times comforting in its routine. A sense of security developed in the routine that kept me on track in the daily grind. I didn't hear the class bell telling me it was time for the next class or that school was out. Instead, I heard the wheels of the buckets the janitorial staff pushed along as they mopped the floors. The housekeeping department would do their thing in my room. They'd empty the wastebasket, mop the floors, dust, and the whole nine yards. I would know that it was mealtime when the cart was rolled near my room and I heard the quick footsteps of the nurse's aides as they passed out the less than mouthwatering meals. In the early morning, I'd hear the best sound ever: my dad getting off the elevator and walking towards my room. He had a gait that I knew well, and the change in his pocket jingled. When he arrived, I knew I was safe for a while. Twice a day, he made that walk. It was always tough to see him go.

I'd been hurt in early May and hadn't finished my fourth quarter for the year. The high school didn't have semesters. A debate ensued among my teachers as to whether I needed to redo the ninth grade. At the time, I was preoccupied with the daily battles, so the school issue brought me back into the reality of life. School was still there; I needed to learn, and I needed to pass to the next grade. In a way, it was a breath of normalcy to be worrying about school again.

After the debate, the principal and the teachers finally concluded that they would let my grades stand and I could move on. Always a goal setter, I had made up my mind that I wanted to finish high school with my class. Their welcome decision kept me in the game and kept me focused on the goal. I was at last thinking about the future and moving on with my life. I didn't realize at the time that there was a lot more in store for me.

Life moved on. Spring football and the accident gave way to the baseball season and missing the team. I did have other victories, though. The tongs in my head were going to be taken out! With that came the discovery that I had a nasty pressure sore on my head and neck area. At one point, they told me I was going to need to take a long deep breath so they could debride the sore, removing the scab. Another battle began.

One guy told me that they would need to give me a shot in my head. Well, my fear of needles didn't help matters. Just the thought of having a needle stuck in my head was more than I wanted to experience again. You know how you feel when you dread doing something? The longer you wait for it to happen, the more fearful you become. The event looms and becomes a formidable pall that hangs over you, like the sword of Damocles. By the time the event arrives, you're living in Anxious City with no car and no bus fare. Basically, you're hosed. Not being able to move my head, I told the guy to just peel off the scab. He came back with something like, "You know this is gonna hurt, right?"

I knew, and I said, "I don't care. Just do it."

So, he started to peel it off. Immediately, I knew I had made the wrong choice. I should have taken the stupid shot. I had compounded the problem and it hurt like hell! After all that, I still have a bald spot where the sore was, a reminder that overcoming your fears is a better route than avoiding them. Something far worse can happen, and it did. Live and learn. Considering the amount of time I had spent in the hospital, I was fortunate that was the only sore I had. One was enough. Other people were not as lucky. I can't imagine having pressure sores all over my body, but some people experience that nightmare.

At the time of my accident, surgery was not an option and the surgical techniques weren't as advanced as they are today. A lot of progress has been made. When hearing about spinal cord injuries, most people envision that the spinal cord was severed. That wasn't true in my case. The spinal cord isn't what most people think it is: a rope, or string-like substance. Rather, the cervical area of the cord is more like an extension of the brain, more malleable than rigid and the area is filled with fluid. When the vertebrae hit against that area, the spinal cord is dislodged, as in my case. That motion causes bruising and swelling and that bruising is what paralyzed me. Sometimes, people are blessed to overcome that problem and the body heals. Unfortunately, that didn't happen with me. The hand I was dealt was different. With the passing of time, scar tissue develops, causing new problems. That was the original great debate while I was still in ER: using fusion, or using traction. Obviously, they opted for traction to pull my neck into alignment.

Now it's possible to cool the area and to inject the site with medication that will reduce swelling and minimize that scar tissue. No doubt injuries like mine motivate doctors to try new therapies. Those therapies naturally were too late in my case, but if medicine adapted and progressed so that other people could find relief, then my injury would at least serve some purpose.

Those injections minimize the damage and, in some cases, help the patient to recover and perhaps even get back on their feet. For me, just being able to move my thumb to my first finger would have been an incredible victory. When you can't do that, life gets a whole lot more complicated. Who would think the inability to make a simple movement would have such consequences in our lives?

Doctors have learned that even after forty years or longer, peripheral nerves can regenerate; however, the spinal cord is the exception. There's no regeneration, and no cure yet. We may have come a long way, but there is still so much progress that is needed. Initially when I got hurt, I couldn't move my arms and hands. I have some movement now, but my hands are still paralyzed. It's better than it could be, and having some arm movement is a whole lot better than none.

It makes me think of my dad prohibiting me from throwing certain pitches in baseball for fear of injury. Turns out, I could have tried to throw those touch pitches—in the end, it wouldn't have mattered if I had been injured, because a more serious injury took its place.

One day, they told me that they were going to take me out of the Stryker frame. I fretted and worried over that big time. I still could feel some pain and the thought of getting out of the frame was terrifying. Yes, the benefit of finally being set free was a positive thing, but fear crept in about what the release would entail. When the tongs were still in place, the doctors continued to add weight to my traction and that pulled on me something awful. The more weight that was added, the more pain I was in. So, I stewed and worried about what was coming with this change. Well, I was in for a surprise. When they pulled the tongs out, I was disoriented again. I hate that feeling and no matter what, there was nothing I could do about it. They still didn't want me to move my neck. No problem there!

I was placed in a Philadelphia collar, which is basically some Styrofoam and Velcro. It wasn't a soft collar by any means. It was rigid with a chin rest and is designed to keep the neck from moving. The wounds where the tongs had been were nasty. They bled quite a bit and the blood dripped down. Now there was something else to conquer. By this time, I really had to work on my mindset. I had to remain determined and resilient. I admit, it was getting tougher to do that. The physical battle was bad enough, but I didn't realize that another, even more formidable battle awaited. Had I known, I don't think I would have fought as hard. I don't think my attitude would have stayed on the positive side. More about that later. Even today, the thought of that new kind of warfare makes me shiver.

For the moment, any thoughts about the world beyond my hospital room quickly faded. Pain can do that in a heartbeat. I was back in the trenches, and I had to dig deeper to keep going.

CHAPTER 10

I finally got out of the Stryker frame and was put into a regular bed, not that that was the ideal situation. They didn't have the technology we do today when it came to hospital beds. Now they have mattresses that move every few seconds, alleviating pressure on the body to eliminate bed sores. Back then, it was just your basic hospital mattress. Someone had to come in regularly and move my legs and me around a bit to keep the sores from developing.

I was finally moved to the rehab unit in another part of the hospital. The hospital was enormous, and the rehab unit took up about six or seven floors. Patients ran the gamut between stroke victims and spinal cord injuries. To me, it was like passing a grade and moving on. I looked forward to something new and hoped that the rehab would be a benefit. Surprises loomed on the horizon. So, off I went to the new unit, sporting my Philadelphia collar and feeling ready to take on the next phase. It was like game day. I no longer wore shoulder pads and a helmet, but I was ready to hit the field and move on.

My parents had needed to make some decisions. After surviving the acute care stage, a decision had to be made about what kind of rehab I would receive. I was just thankful to be in new surroundings, with new walls and a new ceiling to stare at. It's kind of like having a new seating arrangement when you're in grade school. Each quarter, you get a new desk and a new perspective.

Change is good and it was certainly welcome. Progress for me was relative. Life wasn't ever going to be the same, nevertheless, I'd achieved a victory.

I was starting a new adventure and wondered what rehab would be like. At the time, knowing where to find a good rehab facility hadn't even been on the radar. The accident found us woefully unprepared and uninformed about hospitals and treatments. My parents and I were caught up in making it through the next minute, the next hour, and perhaps the day or night. We had won that battle and now faced another.

My parents were introduced to a host of people with whom they could discuss the rehab picture to see where they wanted the next phase to go. They discussed various aspects and kinds of treatment. One person they met, whose name was Ken, had a spinal cord injury. He played football for TCU and knew exactly what I was going through. Apparently, he started a non-profit foundation for spinal cord injuries as result of his unfortunate injury. A lot of positive things can arise from negativity and this was one of them. Ken knew the Texas rehabilitation landscape thoroughly and the landscape in that area was barren. They discussed moving me to another part of the state, but the rehab facility there didn't have the best reputation.

Finally, my parents and their advisors concluded that I should stay where I was so I could be close to family and friends. Not all rehab is physical! It helps to stay close to family and friends in the aftermath of serious injury. My family had been instrumental in keeping me headed in the right direction. They knew me. They understood me, and I understood them. Staying where I was didn't mean that I would be getting better treatment, but I was able to stay near my family. In hindsight, my dad regretted the decision. Indeed, there were much better options elsewhere, but we didn't know it. It didn't become clear in the first few months of rehab. People aren't prepared to make informed decisions for special care.

So, I was moved into the G-Unit, and I don't think the G stood for Good. I was supposed to have a roommate. That certainly helped in having someone else to talk to, someone who was going through similar circumstances. Commiserating can have its benefits, to a point. Up to then, I basically spoke with people who could walk or run anywhere they wanted to go. Having someone in similar circumstances would bring with it an understanding of the reality of the situation. It brought someone who could say, "Yeah, I know what you mean!"

I continued to lose weight and it was an issue. As an athlete and growing boy, my stomach had seemed like a bottomless pit. Not too long ago, my dad told me he didn't know how they kept food in the house for my brother and me. We would eat everything in sight. Consequently, my stomach was a lot larger before the accident, but afterwards, my stomach shrank. Between the unappetizing food and my smaller stomach, food was not appealing, but it was a necessity.

Before the accident, my parents needed to buy four or five chickens for our dinner, which wasn't cheap. I can't imagine paying for all those groceries! I ended up learning how to cut up a whole chicken into various pieces. It was the least I could do considering how much I could eat at that time. At the hospital, I'd have to say that the kitchen's budget wasn't under any threat from me. It certainly wasn't Poncho's Mexican food, and it simply wasn't good.

I started rehab and was wheeled down to the basement to where the rehab equipment was located. To move me from my bed, they had to transfer me to a tilt mat, which was basically a tilting bed. I couldn't be moved very fast. When moved up too fast, the blood would drain from my head and I would pass out! I hated that feeling. It had to be a slow, steady transition. I'm surprised I didn't have to buy a ticket for the tilt bed, like some amusement park ride that would scare you to death! Under normal circumstances, circulation is aided by the muscles in the legs that help to keep things going, but I didn't have that advantage .

When you lie down all the time, changing to a standing position can really shock the body. Healthy people don't need to worry when they hop out of bed in the morning. Their blood pressure is adequate to keep them from passing out. It took me a while to get acclimated and fortunately, they moved me slowly on the tilting bed. Having been tied to the Stryker frame, and then finally released from captivity, my body took a while to catch up when I had to leave my horizontal orientation. Being vertical was a challenge; it took getting used to.

Vertical living brought with it an awareness of my predicament from a different perspective! Once I was upright, I was even more aware of the limitations that lying down had successfully masked. Being vertical made me more keenly aware of a new kind of vulnerability. When you're lying down, areas of vulnerability are apparent, but quasi-standing brought new sensations and the realization that I couldn't just start walking anywhere. The victory of vertical living was overshadowed by the reality of the circumstances. I was just as dependent, or more so, on the people around me in terms of making positional transitions. Being an independent kid who would tear here or there whenever I wanted to—flying solo, if you will—I had to get used to the culture shock of doing things with a great deal of support coming from other people.

In a way, rehab and life in general became a team sport. I had to rely on my "teammates" to do the simplest of things. Fortunately, I had been in a team environment since I was little. That helped in overcoming the feeling that I was helpless. Relying on others requires trust… Knowing that my fellow players had to carry their own weight to propel our team to victory helped me in those awkward and scary moments of trusting other people to help.

Whatever my needs were, I had to totally rely on fellow players. The wheelchair stage was fraught with a lot of passing out. While I wanted to get up and get in the chair so that I could move on with rehab, I still had this unnerving sense that I was going to pass out. For every bit of forward progress, there was an uncomfortable side effect. Someone would have to tilt my wheelchair back until my head was lower than my heart—no small feat. How could I ever drive, or go anywhere? It seemed like I would need an entourage just to wheel down the hall let alone face the looming dangers of the world outside the hospital. Anxiety develops when going through the very things one fears, and for me, passing out was a big one.

It literally took me weeks to get beyond passing out in the wheelchair. Sitting up time was of short duration and it seemed on more than one occasion that I would lose the battle, but I didn't want to be stuck in horizontal hold for the rest of my life. Somehow, I had to overcome the vertical challenges that were daily events. I could tell when I was about to pass out—a function of my heart being unable to get blood and oxygen to my brain. My peripheral vision would gradually be reduced, and my overall sight would narrow to the point that I would only see a bit of light, and I'd be out. It was like driving in the tunnel on IH10 in Mobile, Alabama, feeling the walls closing in until there was complete darkness. It wasn't a panic situation. On the contrary, there was this kind of peaceful feeling, and that was fortunate. Still, it was an awkward thing to go through, and having the team present was preferable in order to reestablish homeostasis. Coming out of it, a point of light would show up and my view expanded. We have prices to pay in life, and learning to sit up had a considerable price tag. I'd be in limbo until someone tilted my chair back enough for me to regain consciousness. However, another problem was ever-present with this remedy: people had to be careful not to tip me back so far that the wheelchair and I would fall over. Such was life.

Things had changed a great deal from the days when I would jump off a roof and land on a trampoline! Getting used to the new me was going to take effort. I wasn't willing to acquiesce in the slightest, but there were difficult times that challenged me to the core. The whole situation was challenging for my family, individually and collectively, but we kept going forward. In thinking about physical therapy, range of motion and strengthening exercises come to mind, but other hurdles must be jumped in order to get that far. Still, I progressed and the range of motion in my legs improved.

When I arrived in the new room in G-Unit, I was the only one there and I got settled. The next day, my roommate, Andy, arrived. He had been hurt about a year and half earlier, suffering a similar spinal cord injury at C-5, so we were already on the same page. He was back in the hospital because of a urinary tract infection—a common thing with the use of catheters—

and the doctors thought he could benefit from PT while there. We could really relate to each other and became fast friends, perhaps aided by our closeness in age. Andy was about nineteen or twenty, just recently out of high school. He had broken up with his girlfriend and shared some personal stories with me, giving me my first glimpse of what life was like in the real world for someone in a wheelchair. His stories were a portal through which I could see a bit of my future.

Our friendship grew. It drew me out of myself, and I began to focus on tomorrow, which made the grueling time in the present seem doable. Our friendship had another positive side effect: our parents got to know each other. For the first time, my parents had a yardstick as to what other parents had experienced; they weren't alone anymore in thinking about problems and issues.

Being a navigator in the Air Force, my dad always had the need to know exactly where he was at any given moment. My accident broke his compass for a while. He struggled with things, as any parent would. Not knowing the new surroundings in which he found himself, and not having access to any "charts" to navigate through the unknown, he must have been stressed. With Andy's parents in the picture, my dad found a map he could use to guide us. He was, after all, the leader of the family, a man upon whom I relied heavily. And my mother could chat with Andy's mom as only two mothers who needed to work through the sufferings of their sons could do. With the knowledge gleaned from Andy and his family, we were able to put a game plan together for the second quarter. The first quarter had been rough, yet armed with knowledge, the future didn't look as bleak or scary.

Andy and I would go to PT together and we had great laughs … I know our laughter had its medicinal qualities. For an hour and a half per day we would go through PT, and then for the rest of the day, we would be back in bed. I still couldn't sit up for long periods without passing out and I still needed help with that. We had an afternoon nurse, Dennis, who came to assist. Dennis was quite the character. I remember times when I was transferred from my chair to the bed and I'd yell out from the pain. Dennis would ask me, "Can you feel that?"

"Yes, dang it. It hurts!"

"Good! Be glad you can feel something," he said.

He had a point.

CHAPTER 11

I mentioned earlier that the hospital I was in was located near downtown Dallas. It was a rough part of town. The rehab area had big bay windows that provided a glimpse into the seamier side of life that went on around the hospital. If we adjusted our beds high enough, or if we were able to be in wheelchairs, we could look down on the interesting happenings below.

In 1980, the drug culture was in full swing, along with prostitution. The neighborhood had a lot of activity and we could see a great deal of it from our hospital window. At times, it was more interesting than TV. Andy and I would turn off the TV and room lights at night, and watch all the activity on the street. An abundance of cars would drive up—people looking for drugs, prostitutes, or both. It was a glimpse into a life that was hard for me to imagine. Even considering everything I was dealing with, I felt lucky. *"Walk a mile in someone's shoes"* kept echoing in my head.

People with problems trying to get their fix one way or the other oozed into the night, attempting to fulfill their needs. After the Vietnam war, a lot of veterans had similar problems. For instance, Dennis, my shift nurse, had a drinking problem. He'd been a triage nurse in Vietnam and must have been fighting some demons and disturbing memories. He would take a drink from a flask every now and then, and the smell of liquor was on his breath all the time. He was a great guy who had obviously seen horrors that haunted him. Such was the case for other veterans who struggled in the aftermath of the war. Coming home to a country where the people were less than hospitable only added fuel to the psychological and emotional fires they fought.

We in rehab had our own issues; we fought them daily, and sometimes won. My weight had become a problem again. I kept losing weight and I kept complaining about the food. Dr. Carter, a man with whom I had difficulty, was after me about my weight. Everything about the guy drove me up a wall. I didn't like him, and as a mouthy fifteen-year-old, I didn't hesitate to tell him so. I never called him doctor, but rather, Mr. Carter. We were like fire and gasoline. I don't know what it was about the man, but I couldn't bring myself to like him. I was chastised by one of the nurses for not showing respect to Dr. Carter. Noted, but to me, respect is earned, and I didn't hesitate to make that point. Perhaps it was based on the angst I felt at the situation, or the accumulation of negativity that went with the accident. Whatever it was, I let the man know I was not fond of him, or his ideas.

He pressed me about eating my lunch. The unappetizing fare sat in front of me, a collection of stomach turning, almost unidentifiable food. I told him

I wasn't going to eat it and that it tasted awful. He told me I needed to eat.

"Do you eat lunch here?" I asked, a bit impertinent.

He looked at me, surprised. Finally, he said, "No." No shock there. I couldn't see anyone who would eat that stuff willingly. He threatened to put a feeding tube in me. Now, I know I needed nourishment—that was obvious. I was skin and bones, but I couldn't get the food down. No one wants to eat stuff that's sickening. Garbage might have tasted better, perhaps with a little hot sauce. Finally, he gave up the battle and left.

After the doctor stormed out, Andy got up and into his wheelchair to look at my tray. He didn't like the food either. He took a spoonful of it and threw it up to the ceiling. The darn spoon stuck to the ceiling and didn't come down. We had a big laugh over that spoon. I was in there for months, and believe it or not, that stupid spoon was stuck to the ceiling the whole time. Whatever was in that food on the spoon, it acted like cement. Maybe some scientist could analyze the compounds: they had to be close to those found in Gorilla Glue.

Andy was a lady's man. He'd wheel out to the nurse's station and chat up the nurses. He started seeing one of the nurses from another floor. She would come to visit him after her shift, getting into bed with him, curtains drawn. Today, nurses would be fired for trying that, but it was another time then.

The time with Andy as a roommate was rather wild. One night, shortly before he left, we were watching a movie on TV. Since we only had one TV, we had to share what stuff we watched. It was about 10:30 p.m. Anyway, we were watching TV and suddenly, we heard this loud crash! We saw a chair fly by the window! It startled us. Who would think you'd see a chair zoom by the window? We were high up. I didn't have my Philadelphia collar on but rather a soft collar that allowed me to turn my head from side to side. Well,

I looked at Andy and he looked at me. We were dumbfounded.

"Did you see that chair?"

"Yeah!"

His answer dispelled any likelihood that I was just seeing things. No sooner had Andy answered me when we saw a bedsheet dangling down by the window, sort of moving in the breeze. Now things were getting interesting.

We were on the fourth floor. On the sixth floor was the psych unit. Someone had tossed a chair through the plate glass window and was trying to escape using bed sheets that were tied together. We could see a guy dangling in front of our window. It was one of those surreal moments that make you blink a few times to make sure you're not seeing things. It was real all right, and that guy was in danger of falling to his death!

When a nurse came in to turn us, Andy said, "Did y'all catch that guy who tried to escape from the floor above us?"

"What are you talking about?" she asked.

"Look out the window!"

She went to the window and saw the sheet blowing back and forth. She ran hell-for-leather out of the room. The strange thing was that nobody on the psych floor even knew someone had tried to escape! How sad is that? That episode broke the monotony, an insidious kind of thing that can drive you batty, especially at fifteen. We were in such a routine on weekdays. Without friends to distract me—they were all too young to drive and couldn't come to visit—the daily grind of the hospital life became our "normal" day.

To say that human beings are adaptable is an understatement. We can and do adapt to new situations, new routines, and a change in lifestyles—eventually.

However, it doesn't happen easily at first. Just like I did, most of us create a fuss, mouth off a bit, and often wait to be dragged into our new reality, but in the end, we do adapt. We must adapt, and you know, if you can learn to go with the flow, no matter how weak or strong the current is, it will take us where we need to be. We may pass through pain, sorrow, anger, and desperation, but if we take a deep breath and ride it out, we get to a place where we can cope, a place where we can live. Sure, significant changes may be forced on us: it's all part of life. Dropping our resistance to change can come naturally, or we may let go of our resistance when too fatigued to put up a fight and subsequently discover that life goes on.

A quasi-comfort zone is established, and we find we can cope. I'm not saying we don't have days or weeks of inner turmoil and upsets, but a comfort zone will be found in which we can live.

I found mine…but it wasn't permanent, and to be honest, if we stay in a comfort zone too long, we get complacent and growth is stunted. If we use the time spent in a comfort zone to recoup and to heal and not to malinger, we are much more prepared to move on; we *should* move on. We must grow and meet the challenges that present themselves, the golden opportunities that life brings us, however frequent or painful.

Andy was my roommate for just a short time. He went on his way and I never really knew what happened to him. He was a resilient guy and I trust he got along well. My next roommate, Steve, had a spinal cord injury. Steve was married to a nice woman named Donna. They were from Austin, Texas. Steve had been injured in a diving accident. He was at a party and dove into the swimming pool, breaking his neck. He was young and had his whole life ahead of him. Like me, he was thrust into a challenge.

Steve had graduated from the same high school I'd gone to in Garland. He was a few years older, but we got along. Our common situation helped, and it also helped to have another roommate. Donna was a real character. She was Southern, with a pronounced drawl. She and Steve were diehard Texas fans. Naturally, my Oklahoma paraphernalia was the subject of contention, good natured to be sure, but we were on opposite sides of the fence when it came to football. In forty years, I haven't missed one OU game, whether I watched it on TV, heard it on the radio, or went in person. I disliked Texas just as much as they disliked Oklahoma. It made for some interesting times, particularly when the two teams faced one another. As I got to know the couple better, we felt comfortable enough to chide each other about the teams. Our rivalry became just as big as the schools themselves. In a way, it was fun.

Steve had undergone a tracheotomy, just like Christopher Reeves. His tube was finally removed, and he could breathe on his own. He hadn't had it out for long, so Donna needed to put her finger over the hole so that Steve could talk. It was a big struggle for him to talk and to breathe. They put him on breathing exercises. Like me, he developed a pressure sore, a large one, but his was on his butt. It was so large and nasty that it had to be packed with gauze. He had other issues too. Overall, I counted my blessings because I was in much better shape than Steve.

We were roommates for about three months and you get to know people well under those circumstances. We both needed to have nurses come in and turn us side to side every two hours to keep pressure sores at bay. One night, we waited to be turned, but no nurse came in. We were stuck lying on our sides the entire night. I had one hip area that turned red and so did Steve.

The next morning, just as he always did, my dad came in with my McDonald's hash browns, the only thing I wanted to eat. I was crying. He asked what the problem was, and I told him we had been stuck on our sides the whole night. Tears streamed down my face. My dad pulled back the sheets and saw that the side of my hip and butt was red. He carefully removed the pillow between my knees and turned me to the other side. He went over to Steve and did the same. Then, he went ballistic.

He marched down to the nurse's station and raised hell. I could hear him from my room. He asked to see the administrator. When the administrator showed up, he asked him, "Why haven't these boys been turned all night?" My dad was angry, and you didn't mess with him when he got that way. Well, the nurse who should have turned us was on duty that same evening and Hell hath no fury like a nurse who's been royally chewed out.

She came in that evening and screamed at Steve and me. That woman was really ticked off. Then she made some chilling comments that not only removed us from our comfort zone, but placed us in the crosshairs. "If you ever tell on me again, I'll kink your catheters so your urine won't flow, and you'll get dysreflexia." We weren't taught much in rehab there, but we were told that if our catheters were blocked and we couldn't empty our bladders, our bodies would sense something was terribly wrong. Blood pressure would rise dramatically, and we would have strokes and die.

Her words were frightening and I'm sure our eyes bugged out as she ranted. In no uncertain terms, she threatened us, and let me tell you, the fear we felt was palpable. You know when someone is serious: you know they mean what they say. This woman appeared to have meant every word. I won't say I knew what was in her heart, but I sure recognized an overt threat when I heard one. On top of that, what could Steve or I do to defend ourselves? Put up a fight? That wasn't going to happen—we were helpless. Now, more than ever, we felt totally at the mercy of this woman who was no

Florence Nightingale. She put the character, Annie, in Stephen King's *Misery* to shame!

We believed what she said. I really think she believed it too. Dreadful trepidation hit us. What would happen if we drifted off to sleep? Would we ever wake up? Other things crossed our minds that only made the terror worse. If we dared to talk about the threat, we would be putting our lives on the line. We were in a terrible quandary. Of course, your mind makes things worse when you mull the possibilities. This was like living in a horror movie and we were the potential victims. With night approaching, our fears burgeoned, our minds and hearts racing with a hideous, disconcerting feeling that we couldn't shake.

What if…?

CHAPTER 12

To this day, I still have apprehension when I think about my catheter kinking or getting pinched. That nurse had both of us trapped in a bad situation. Even worse, she knew it and used it to her advantage. She might as well have pointed a gun at us. Every night she would come in and roughly turn us side to side, mumbling under her breath before storming out of the room.

Making waves isn't always the best thing to do, especially in a hospital setting. The vulnerability I felt was profound and I hated how I felt. I thought long and hard about saying something. I knew my parents would move me out of that rehab in a heartbeat, perhaps to another city. That would put me further from friends and family, creating an even tougher burden on my everyone. Besides, Steve had come from another hospital that he deemed even worse — a hospital where he got a nasty bedsore and had a hole in his throat from a tracheostomy: no thanks!

Each time my dad stepped off the elevator, morning and evening, and I heard him walking towards my room, I thought that I would and should say something to him. Naturally, I was relieved to hear him coming. He made things better for me. I was also relieved that I'd made it through the night. Yet, the terror continued. Each time my dad came into the room, I wanted to tell him, to whisper to him what the nurse told us. I knew he would reach critical mass in a heartbeat. I didn't know what would happen. If he went to the hospital administrator as he did when that other nurse didn't turn us all night, the repercussions would be awful. They could prove deadly.

Even if they fired the nurse, she could still come back and kink the catheters (or who knows what) in our sleep! Not being able to stop the nurse physically, we pondered the possibilities of what we could do. A pall came over me during my dad's visits. Instead of focusing on our talks, I had an inner debate going on. *Should I tell him or not?* I longed to tell him. So, my attention was divided. My dad knows me better than anyone, and I don't know if he picked up on it or not, but I ate my McDonald's hash browns, just like always, and decided to keep quiet.

That decision made things worse. Things were now left with Steve and me to resolve, or die trying. Death seemed likely. Heck, it would have been murder. Each day, exhausted from lack of sleep and the terror of the unknown associated with that nurse, we had a brief respite knowing that nighttime was still several hours away. I was so relieved when my dad visited, but he left all too soon. By evening, fear took hold and it felt like we were dangling from a jagged precipice, holding on with just a couple of fingers. At any moment, we might succumb.

Even if we could somehow drift off to sleep, the slightest noise was a portent of what could happen. To me, it was like camping in rattlesnake country. Quiet and deadly, you didn't know when one would strike. I really think I had PTSD from that episode and to some extent still suffer from that abuse. We struggled through the night and by early morning, I longed to hear that elevator ding and my dad's pockets jingle with the coins in his pockets with every footstep because I knew I would be all right. After about a couple of weeks of this, the nurse was gone. Maybe her deeds finally caught up with her or she got another job; I don't really know. I just know she was gone, and I never saw her again. I never realized until then that a person so entrusted with a loved one's care could be so cruel. The emotional damage must feel similar for those who are habitually bullied today. The fear, humiliation, and sense of vulnerability created scarring that stays with you forever. I was fifteen when this happened, but I will live with it forever. I hear today this type of abuse still goes on, particularly in nursing home facilities.

My dad and I never discussed these events until recently. It was during the writing of this book that I broached the subject. Forty years had gone by but he remembered the incident well. I finally mentioned it, and the veil of threats I was under. Of course, he was not too happy about it. He said he'd had no idea about the fear I was living through. Whether it was divine intervention or pure determination, we made it—not without scars, though. Sometimes those scars open and the fear returns. That was true when I broke my leg and had to have surgery a few years ago, and again more recently with bladder surgery. How I hate entering a hospital situation! Looking back, I refuse to let one bad apple spoil the memories of the many caring and wonderful people I've encountered. I guess you could say I've seen the best and worst of mankind.

Anyway, we got through it and there were lighter moments. By October, the football season was in full swing. I had been able to go home on weekends for visits, which was wonderful, particularly because that nurse was nowhere in sight! Let me tell you, I didn't rush back to the hospital after those weekends at home. I'd get back at the very last minute.

On one of those weekends there was the Oklahoma/Texas football game! Steve's wife, Donna, had given me a hard time as game day got closer. They both were such rabid Texas fans and there I was on my side of the room, which was bedecked in OU red. The joshing was good natured, and occasionally, there were some sharper comments. I was always the kid in the red OU shirt. It didn't bother me. Sadly, Texas beat OU that year—I guess it was just one of those things. It was my time to eat crow, but my love for OU never wavered. I dreaded going back to the hospital on Sunday, knowing full well Steve and Donna would give me heck over the game. I expected them to be playing the victors, sitting in the catbird seat. Being the brunt of their teasing was expected. What are friends for, right?

I delayed the inevitable, leaving home late. My dad and I got to the hospital and I got checked in and went to my room. The lights were out. I thought maybe I'd escaped the anticipated chastisement. I was wrong. Donna had put up burnt orange streamers on my side of the room and my sheets and pillowcases were now burnt orange! Even though my dad was a huge Oklahoma fan, he thought it was hilarious! However, for me, it was a devastating moment, and not just because of Oklahoma's loss to Texas. I started bawling, hard. I cried and cried.

"What happened?" my perplexed dad asked. So many emotions had hit me all at once, some realizations hitting home with painful accuracy. I thought I had come to terms with my situation, but I think in the back of my mind, I still had hope that I would walk again. I thought I would play football again. For the first time, it really hit me that I would not be doing those things, and it shook me up badly. In that awful moment, I realized I would never play for OU. I would never again take to the field, and battle with my opponents on the other side of the line. It was over. My dreams died that night as I looked at the burnt orange trappings on my side of the room. I was brokenhearted.

Looking back on it, I think that meltdown was a conglomeration of all the emotions, all of the pain and rehabilitation that followed the accident. At fifteen, relegated to a wheelchair for life, my existence was forever altered. It was quite a moment. Teenagers can blow things out of proportion and see things far more dramatically than they really are. Nevertheless, in that moment of shocking realization, I knew my dream had burst.

Every second weekend in October, I still watch the Texas/OU football game. It's bittersweet, and often painful, but I'm a diehard OU fan and always will be. As I watch the OU players running out of the tunnel and hitting the field, I think about my dream of doing the same thing. I never got the chance to run out of the tunnel with the team amidst the din and roar of the OU stadium fans.

I realize now, looking through the lens of time, that the odds of me getting an offer to play football at the collegiate level were probably low. With the thousands of kids that play high school football, only a small percentage play at the next level. Still, it was my dream and I had laid out a game plan to get there. Even with the best of plans and aspirations, life has a way of changing directions much like a leaf bounces off tree limbs on its descent to the ground. I could have been one of those guys, all juiced up to play Texas ... I *should* have been one of those guys, but it didn't happen. In a way, I suppose that burnt orange bomb that exploded that Sunday night was a blessing. I hit bottom then, and I hit it with a mighty thud. I was tackled, and if there had been a referee in the room, he might have called "Piling On." I was down, falling far short of the end zone. It was a hard hit, the kind that leaves turf stuck to the facemask of your helmet.

The harsh reality made me realize that in hitting rock bottom, there was no place else to go but up. Just like in football, I would have to fight my way forward, trying to gain yardage. Life was showing me its red zone defense, and somehow, I had to find a way to achieve my goals. At that moment, I didn't have a set of goals, but I quickly formed them. I would go back to school. I would graduate with my class. I would learn how to drive, and I would go on to college, not on a football scholarship, but on the scholarship of desire to succeed. Now more than ever, I had to succeed. I had to find my way in life and be the best I could be.

Instead of wearing the OU uniform, I would don a new one, of sorts. Instead of running down and tackling the ball carrier, I would have to step up and be the quarterback of my life, calling my plays as best I could. Sure, the sidelines would have its medical personnel, its coaches sending in plays of what to do next. Yet, in the heat of battle, and the new reality of my life, I vowed to rely on my own plays, win, lose, or draw.

Amid the burnt orange, I also saw red that Sunday night, and although I would never walk down the OU tunnel, I did see a faint light at the end of my own tunnel. I knew that with hard work and perseverance, I would reach the light at the end of that tunnel. I knew I might not hear the cheers of the crowd, but I would try to win each step of my future until I achieved my goal.

That devastating night set me on a new path, but not an easy one. At the time, I couldn't imagine the trials that lay ahead—all I knew was that I had to take them on.

It wasn't long after this that I was informed I would soon be going home. The realization that I would be released from the hospital brought many logistical challenges. The biggest was the accessibility of our house. The weekend passes home had given us a glimpse of the changes needed for doors, bathrooms, and even in terms of getting into our house. It was a huge project and expense. Once again, neighbors and friends came to the rescue. A Little League coach I barely knew was a contractor and quickly came to help. Mr. Colburn and his sons worked nights and weekends converting a bedroom and adding a bathroom, all accessible for my wheelchair. All materials were donated and all labor provided free of charge. How can words even begin to describe how grateful we felt? The power of kindness is truly a humbling thing.

* * *

Mom was packing my belongings into a box. I was sitting in my wheelchair, staring out that big bay window in my hospital room, looking at the traffic and people hurrying by as they got on with their busy day. I thought about my place in this new world of mine. Rehab, even with all its issues, seemed comforting compared to the real world. The unknown scared me, and I began to sob and cry. Puzzled, my mom asked, "What's wrong, Jim?"

"How will I fit in that world? I'm so different now."

In her reassuring voice, she said, "We will take it one day at a time and I know you will do it." With that, she packed the remaining items and I rolled out the door into my new reality.

CHAPTER 13

As a kid, even as young as ten years old, I was a problem solver. In the serious situations that arose following my accident, it was problem solving that helped me get through things; it was a way out of adversity. Sure, there were times that I couldn't think beyond the moment, but as things progressed, I was able to concentrate on the problems at hand and work through them.

If I had been stranded on a deserted island at age ten, and had to choose one other person to be there with, my answer might surprise you ... I know it surprised me. The average ten-year-old might immediately say they'd want to be stuck on an island with a famous sports hero or actor. While those choices might be great, they weren't mine. I guess I'd have to say I'd pick my parents, but if I could only have one other person to be stranded with, it would come down to my dad. My mom would probably freak out at hearing this. I was close to her as a boy, but you must remember that I always analyzed things (and still do), so choosing my dad would have made the most sense. Under the duress of being stuck on an island, my dad had the skills needed for us to survive. He would know how to build a shelter, light a fire and keep it going, and find food. In other words, he would analyze the situation and find a solution. We're a lot alike in many ways.

That was fortunate, because it was the ability to solve problems that enabled my resiliency. I was able to work out solutions, and trust me, there were plenty of problems to solve. When you're stuck in a hospital room, not able to move, you have a lot of time to think. The better I felt, the more I thought about things, and so many things cropped up that needed to be addressed. How was I going to do this or that? What am I going to do about school, or even the smallest of tasks? Admittedly, getting lost in your own thoughts can have its downside. Overanalyzing gives rise to doubt, fear, and worrying about the unknown—I admit I'm guilty of this, and it can have the same crippling effect as the situation I cope with each day.

The only other person I can think of who I would care to be stranded with was my best friend, Randy. We got along so well. We pushed each other to be the best, and just as my older brother Robbie did, he had my back. At ten years old, neither of us suspected what was to come. I had a core group of great high school friends, but Randy was instrumental upon my return to high school. He was there for me.

By the time I was released from hospital, it was well into the fall semester of my sophomore year. I started homebound school lessons with a teacher assigned to come by my house three days a week. If you imagined rehab to be boring, this was worse—at least the hospital environment was an active one with people constantly coming and going, helping to break up the day. Being cooped up at home felt like house arrest. The initial plan was for me to be a homebound student for my entire sophomore year. I was already behind in the required work, and the thought of repeating a grade just made the situation worse. When I told my parents that I wanted to go back to school full time, I think they questioned whether I could handle the long days. My sitting tolerance was not that great, even after six months. I had lost 67 pounds in the hospital, and I was skin and bones. Even my physical appearance had changed so much that I did not look like the same guy. After some discussions with both school staff and family members, we agreed that I would try returning on a trial basis after Christmas break in January of 1981.

Going to class had its own set of issues for me. First, it was tough not knowing how I'd be accepted. The challenges of traversing the campus and getting to classes also brought anxiety. In addition, I had to figure out how to get from one class to another on time. As it turned out, I'd often need to leave class early to get where I had to be, but Randy, Brian, Rodney, and a host of other guys would leave with me—they loved leaving early! What kid wouldn't? They'd help me down the hallway of our two level school. Fortunately, the school had an elevator; unfortunately, you had to have a key to open the elevator door. Now, unlocking the door and opening it, shutting it, and then pushing the buttons isn't that big a deal ... unless, of course, you're in a wheelchair with limited hand movements. Timing was everything. The way schedules worked out, I didn't always have the guys with me, so in trying to maintain some semblance of normalcy, I attempted to navigate on my own.

Using the elevator key was a problem. My dad figured out a way to make a key holder (which I wore on a cord around my neck) so that I could insert it by myself. After that, I was able to negotiate my way in and out of the elevator more easily. I did manage to get stuck a few times when things went south. Fortunately, the elevator had an alarm button for summoning help.

Those first few weeks of going to school were exhausting. I didn't have an electric chair, and muscles that had lost their strength rebelled at first, but after a while, I built up my strength. My options for building up physical exercise were now very different: I could no longer use the weight room, run wind sprints, or play catch. Faced with these kinds of changes, a mental wall can come down, limiting the view of the road ahead, and when you keep hitting obstacles, you wonder if you should even try to go forward. Eventually, my problem-solving kicked in and my drive to achieve goals gave me a strength and courage I didn't know I had. I kept on moving ahead. Sure, it was at a different pace, using a different method, but nevertheless, I kept moving.

I had hard moments at times when trying to problem-solve. Even thinking through things was tough because anticipating all the problems or situations in order to prepare for them is impossible. Randy was always there for me, and it helped. When I would try and weasel out of things, he would step in and say: "Hell no, you're doing it." He stuck with me every step. I can't say that after the accident we picked things up right where we left off. Things had obviously changed dramatically, but not so our friendship; we still talk today. Randy was the kind of guy I could talk to, telling him things I couldn't or wouldn't tell somebody else, not even my family. After the accident, there were many things that needed talking out and Randy was there. Everyone needs someone like that. You know the old saying that you really know who your friends are when times are tough? It's true, and I sure found that out. Randy, along with Brian, Rodney, and a couple of other guys too, hung in there with me. I was much more confident knowing that I was not alone in my new world.

Through it all, my dad continued to be my role model, giving me the security I needed to go forward. It was like learning to ride a bike again. My dad had his hands on the bike as I wobbled down the sidewalk. Once I got better, he only kept one hand on the seat. Before I knew it, I was doing well—feeling more sure of myself, but still content to know that my dad was hanging on. Yet, there came a moment when I stole a look behind me to find out that my dad was ten yards back, and I had managed to ride all alone. In a way, I was back at square one after the accident. I needed to relearn how to do things, to ride a virtual bike with training wheels, so to speak, counting on my dad to be there to steady me and to guide me.

One never knows at the time how seemingly small, random events can be such a powerful force for change and good in someone's life. I had a very positive experience with Kent, a guy in a wheelchair who came to visit me in the hospital. He'd been hurt playing football, so we had that connection from the start. I mentioned that getting my driver's license was on my radar before my accident and mumbled about that dream being over. Then Kent told me he could drive, and I couldn't believe it. Hope was ignited! He arranged for me to go down to the parking lot and he brought his van around front. He showed me how he got in his modified van, and immediately, my analytical side kicked in. It occurred to me that he had the same level of spinal cord injury as me, and if I worked at it, I could get my driver's license too and not miss that all-important rite of passage. What teenager doesn't want to drive? A driver's license and a car are symbols of freedom!

I had bemoaned not being able to reach that goal, but after seeing Kent with that van, and looking at the hand controls making it possible for him to drive, I knew I could do it. In a real way, I was reborn: just because your body is injured doesn't mean you don't have the same desires and dreams that everyone else has. Granted, those desires haven't always proved attainable, but in this case, boy howdy, they were possible!

Of course, I needed to build up my strength to achieve the goal of driving. My sixteenth birthday was coming up in April, and my father had investigated getting me into adaptive driving training at a local facility in the spring of 1981. A plan was put in place and I knew in my heart I could do it; I'd be damned if anyone told me differently. Everyone needs that kind of motivation and goal, and things didn't seem as dark after that. I had found a means of going places and gaining independence, something every teen longs for. At the time of my accident, I was just at the point of getting my learner's permit, and the future had seemed bright and exciting. Okay, I'd had a big detour, but I was now back on course.

To every guy at that age, cars and girls were ever on the brain. I had hoped I'd drive soon, but girls? It didn't seem like they'd be on my radar, no matter how hard I wished. One day, that all changed. We all have random events that happen in our lives that might seem insignificant or trivial to others. After an accident like mine, body image can be a big deal. The wheelchair, muscle atrophy, and untimely, uncontrollable intestinal gas weigh on an individual, especially in social situations. I really had to find ways to overcome such burdens on my mental health. As with so many other times in my life, I used humor to mask my self-consciousness. While I was still in the hospital, something unforgettable happened that changed my outlook.

A local TV show was running a story about me, checking on my progress and catching up with me in rehab. The TV channel was following up on a *Dallas Morning News* article about me and were going to air a feature spot on a show called *PM Magazine*. Well, I was doing my physical therapy thing, trying to improve my range of motion and build up some strength. The TV crew filmed me going through my workout. I noticed that during it all, a girl was watching me … It caught me off guard. She seemed interested in me and I picked up on it; however, I quickly dismissed it. Why would she be interested in me, a guy in a wheelchair?

"Hey, that girl's been asking about you the past couple of days," a therapist said.

"Interested in me?" I still dismissed it.

"Why don't I push you over and you can talk to her?"

I was told her mother had experienced a stroke and was now going through rehab. It was summer, so she was there every day. I thought about it. Before I was injured, I wouldn't have hesitated; now things were different. But I analyzed the situation and thought, "What do I have to lose?" I went over and talked to her. We hit it off. Over the next two weeks, she would visit me in my room. It was great to have her company! She would stay most of the day until someone came to pick her up at three or four in the afternoon. Sometimes, she would lie down on the bed and we'd watch TV. We did what kids our age did: we held hands, and we made out a bit. That lasted about two weeks, and then she stopped coming by the hospital. Our relationship was very positive for me, helping me a great deal. To be honest, I think we helped each other. I never talked to her again, but I knew at that point I was going to be okay! Driving, and dating were possible! Life took a positive turn! Motivated to be the best I could be, I knew I needed to do more to turn my life around.

The Dallas hospital did its job on several levels, but it really fell behind when it came to comprehensive rehabilitation. After my parents realized that there were rehab facilities outside of our community, they explored the situation. The hospital in Houston, as I mentioned earlier, wasn't the best place for me. At this point, I had to regroup in order to recoup, and to find a rehab that would help me in ways the Dallas hospital could not. After my return to high school in the spring, my family and I realized that there was much more to learn about my disability. So, after more research and recommendations, I ended up at Craig Hospital in Denver, a magnet hospital specializing in brain and spinal cord injuries.

Being at Craig was a game changer. It opened my eyes and opened doors for me that would put me on the right track for life. While my rehab had been minimal in Texas, Craig provided a comprehensive approach. I didn't know it at the time, but I was badly in need of their expertise and help. Only getting the bare necessities in Dallas, I was encouraged when I saw the game plan at Craig. Talk about a team approach! Many healthcare professionals came together to assist with the task of regaining life and dignity.

Although I still analyzed things, I didn't realize that I was going through a grieving process. Following the accident, I wasn't seen by a psychologist in Dallas. No one explained to me that I had to go through the various stages of grief. I knew I was going through the pain and reality of the accident, but I didn't know about the grieving process—a normal thing for anyone who goes through a crisis, particularly a crisis that changes your life so drastically from one moment to the next.

My grieving process was much the same as it is for people who lose loved ones. I lost the use of my legs. My arm function was greatly diminished. Since my Oklahoma dream died on our practice field, I lost football too. A person doesn't just wake up the next morning after such a critical event and say, "Oh, well ...." The following days and months require working through the changes, and that means a time of mourning.

When emotions and pain are stifled, that can lead to many things, including harm to one's physical and emotional health. Making matters worse, mental health was not a common topic in the late 70s and early 80s. I had watched the movie, "One Flew Over the Cuckoo's Nest" (no thanks!) so I resisted help at first, but after some coaxing, I relented. I was able to talk to a psychologist at Craig and to work through things. Craig and its staff were instrumental in showing me that it was possible to live a full life, albeit somewhat altered, but a productive life nevertheless.

Rehab can be grueling; my time in Denver proved that. Still, I learned how to function in the world. Through occupational and physical therapy, counseling, and real-life experiences, I developed the skills, and eventually the confidence, to get on with my life.

CHAPTER 14

In looking back at the coping mechanisms I had or didn't have at the time of my accident, I found one constant that always remained in play. Sometimes, its presence may have slipped to the back of my mind, but underneath all the turmoil, the stress, and the pain, my parents had laid a foundation for me to succeed despite the many trials, and times of adversity. In particular, my father reinforced in his offspring daily both the value and meaning of real-world experiences. We weren't coddled or spoiled by any means, and we were taught to handle things as they came. Learning responsibility for our actions was at the top of the list. Sometimes, those lessons have to be learned the hard way, but where better to learn them than at home?

I was brought up to believe that the world never owed me anything: everyone earns his or her own way and we all put in our time, doing the best we possibly can at any given moment. With this kind of upbringing, my father also reinforced the fact that the world was a tough place, which was certainly brought home to me after my accident when I learned just how tough things could get. If I had been spoiled and hadn't learned coping skills through real-life applications, I think the trauma would have been far worse. Sure, there were moments when I felt down, and felt a little sorry for myself. However, my parent's maxims and how they lived their lives gave me the strength to keep going. Sometimes, it would have been much easier to be so consumed with self-pity that I would have been just as immobile mentally and emotionally as I was physically, but I persevered.

My parents didn't rush to the rescue when we messed up; we were taught to figure things out on our own. If parents always intervene, children never really take off their emotional and mental training wheels. We were not the perfect family, but what family is? We had our share of misunderstandings, strong wills, sibling fights, arguments—oh, the arguments. But I'm glad my parents were the way they were. I knew that I had to depend on myself, and if I forgot something, it was my fault. I didn't expect my parents to drop everything in order to fix my problem. I'm not saying that I didn't need help, especially after my accident; I did, and I counted a great deal on the support I received from my parents. Yet, in time, I again reached that spot where I could step up and figure things out for myself.

One of my best traits is resiliency: that determination to get back up when we are knocked on our ass. We all need it, but not all of us have it. I had a healthy dose of it and it certainly helped after the accident. I had been tackled, but I had to get up quickly, and get back in the game. Physically, the game had changed big time; my mental game, anchored by resiliency, was now all important. Fortunately, I am resilient. If I weren't, it might have been all over. Other people see that resiliency in me more readily than I do; I'm not sure why. It's true that I've always loved challenges (they bring out the best in me) and that the accident put that to the test. When challenges arrive, we can meet them head on, side-step them, or run away. I chose to work through the challenges in my life. The tougher they were, the harder I tried to conquer them.

Well-meaning people often try to help by saying, "Hey, you can't do that!" My response to that was: "Watch me!" I kept that attitude throughout the ordeal, through rehab and the rest of my life. Being told I couldn't do something just made me more determined to do it. Failures? You bet … I've had more than my share. Most of the time, I've proven people wrong. I *can* do things; I *can* succeed.

Battles involving my worthiness were harder after the accident, especially having to deal with people from the vantage point of my wheelchair. Preconceived notions get in the way. People's perspectives of disabled people often prove that there are other disabilities in the world, even among the seemingly healthy. The skewed views that people form end up doing the disabled person a huge disservice. In fact, those views can be more crippling than the disability itself.

Those of us with physical limitations are put to the test in society. To succeed, we must overcome obstacles, and often that means overcoming other people's narrowmindedness and/or fears. This was especially true before the passage of The Americans with Disabilities Act, or ADA. When you have a disability, as I found out, you must push harder, be tougher, smarter, and more capable than circumstances would normally demand. It's unfair in a way, but for me, I used that to my advantage. Of course, being in sports is a competitive thing, and I was still in a completely competitive frame of mind after my accident. I needed to prove to the world and to myself that I was no worse off than anyone else. The only problem is that the very nature of disabilities puts undulations and hurdles on a normally level playing field. I had to forget "normal"! I now had a new sense of normality, and I worked to achieve all I could. In all of this, sometimes people get in each other's way. As I worked through my disability, it not only challenged me, but also the people around me.

At one time or another, we all reach out for acceptance from people—we need it. Acceptance can validate us as individuals and help us acquire confidence. For the disabled, finding acceptance can be harder. I was accepted by my family, of course, but being accepted in the larger world was another matter. Some of that stemmed from my own issues, but overall, I felt like I had to earn acceptance from others around me. During this process, a phobia of sorts can develop, one which can lead to too much introspection—like looking at your life under a microscope rather than at the world around you. Always quick to critique myself, whether in sports or in life generally, I found out that I could be very hard on myself. It's taken me a long time, years in fact, to know that I can't always win people's acceptance. I've struggled with my worthiness in relation to other people and sometimes come up short. Incidents in my life underscored that so completely that I still need to work through things today. The struggles continue, and I suspect they will continue until I die. Over the years, I have come to terms with things, and within the past couple of years, I have found peace about not being accepted. Although it's been hard for me to understand why I haven't been accepted, I've learned to accept myself. I don't know if my inability to accept myself was an impediment that people picked up on or not. Nevertheless, I'm more comfortable in my own skin now.

After the accident, I carried a heavy burden about all this, one that was sometimes overwhelming. Having always been hard on myself, the lack of approval from other people made me beat myself up more. We all want people to accept us for who we are. When you don't get acceptance, a person might try to mold their persona to fit it. I finally came to the realization that the acceptance issues weren't really inside me, but rather inside other people. I had taken on the weight of their disapproval—all wrapped up in their perception of me—and that wasn't the way it was supposed to be. I needed to be authentic, despite having failed frequently to do so. That would be the only way to feel accepted for who I was.

Society has changed a great deal in the years following my accident; it's become a world where we are judged by our appearances rather than for who we are. We're led to believe that we must act a certain way, live a certain way; conform, fit in, and be attractive. Those are the messages given off by advertisers, and people in general. Our culture has been divided, subdivided, and torn apart by appearances with the category you land in depending on the views of others.

I'll be the first to admit that I have battled depression off and on for years. It's a tough battle with a foe that can be oppressive, consuming, and unrelenting. Things can chip away at our psyches, our fragile veneer, making things worse. It's like Chinese water torture! The constant drip, drip, drip of pain, unhappiness, and lack of acceptance and approval can exact a big toll. If I hadn't been resilient, I never would have made it.

I managed to graduate from high school, and learned to drive a car. College was on the horizon and I really wanted to pursue my education. I never expected to be looking at college in a different light: never did I imagine I'd be hobbled and in a wheelchair. The bright lights of the football field were dimmed, but I learned to accept that. Before entering college, I had another period of retrospection. If I'd had a time machine, and was able to go back to a time in my past, I would have picked my eighth grade year at Webb Middle School, a particularly good year for me. I had a girlfriend; I was doing well in school, and I played football. Sitting in my wheelchair, I thought back to the end of that particular year. We were at an assembly, waiting to see who would get the All Webb Award. I was in my OU jersey, happy to be there, and excited to move on to the next big thing.

I wondered who would win the prestigious award. To my surprise, they called my name! I had no idea I was even being considered for the award! What a shock! The teachers had to nominate the students they thought were deserving. Now, I've got to tell you, I was no straight-A student. I studied Texas history that year. Math was not my strong suit. As for English, I did all right for that, but I just couldn't imagine I'd be in the running. So, winning the award literally came out of left field. I received a plaque that day and it was one of those things that really stuck out in my mind. I kept the plaque on the wall in my room, partially because I was fond of the last line engraved on it: "A person all will aspire to be like," or something to that effect.

In that moment of retrospection, I wondered if anybody would aspire to be like me now. Basically, I was the same person I'd always been, except for one thing: the wheelchair. Inside, I was still me. Times and people change. We all have awards we like to win. Often, we don't get the recognition or awards we would like. My dad used to say that even being nominated is an award by itself. So, it was blessed indeed—a blessing that came at the end of a magical year.

In thinking about awards, and as a football player, you'd think that I would like to have won the Heisman Trophy, football's pinnacle achievement. I played so many positions in football, not really sticking to one in particular. It never occurred to me that I might be eligible for the Heisman, like Billy Sims, for instance. To me, football was a team sport and that was fine with me. Even if someone from Oklahoma U had won the Heisman, to me it would still be due to the team working together, making it possible for the individual who won the award. For example, running backs need blockers; without them, a running back could easily be tackled behind the line of scrimmage.

College brought its own set of challenges, some difficult and some surprisingly positive. I still had to navigate the campus and get to class. I met a lot of friends there, some closer than others. Personally, I was satisfied to be part of the team. Many of the college and NFL greats who achieved great success were really spoiled brats whose bad behavior ended up destroying their careers. When we only hear raves about our performance and we get news coverage and fame, we can lose sight of where we need to improve—getting kudos and recognition are only good to a point. If you start reading your own press clippings, the hype can turn your head and mess with your ego. We all need to hear that we still have work to do, that we still need to change this or that. We need to keep working harder— it's what keeps us grounded. Perhaps that's why I was always so hard on myself. I always wanted to improve; I felt that I needed to do better.

The trouble with many athletes is that they get into partying too hard, but it's so counterproductive to drink and do drugs. When I was in high school, alcohol was the drug of choice. Some kids did weed, but booze was at the top of the list. To be honest, drugs scared the hell out of me. In high school, we had parties every weekend and for me, that meant drinking. At first, I drank to fit in, and after the accident that was probably still true, if not to a greater degree.

Those parties often led to binge drinking. Kids would be clean all week, but come Friday and Saturday night, it was time to party hard. Everybody was drinking, and so when in Rome, you do what they do to fit in. However, it became more than that: it became an escape, a getaway that led me out of my situation for a while. Yet, it was destructive, and it's not something I am proud of about that particular time in my life because I put myself, and sometimes others, at risk with my behavior.

I'm glad social norms today are much harsher towards teenage drinking. It is simply not worth ruining lives over self-indulging in alcohol. Drinking aside, I am eternally grateful to the students and teachers at North Garland. They welcomed me back with open arms. Doc, the trainer who rushed to my aid when I first got hurt, gave me an honorary position on his training staff to keep me engaged with the football team. The Class of '83 was one of a kind. Overcoming adversity was the theme our senior year when a couple of students tragically passed away before graduation. We pulled together as class, just as we did when I was injured, and we helped each other out. Here's to the Class of '83!

CHAPTER 15

As mentioned, goal setting has always been important to me, even as a kid. Graduating from high school with my class was a big achievement even without the challenges I faced. My circumstances could have put that goal out of reach, but being determined to meet it, I pushed myself on many different levels to get there.

Like many young people, once that goal was met, I had my sights set on college. It was the next step on the way to my new reality. Indoctrinated quickly into this world after the accident, and despite the jarring aftermath, I wanted to keep my goals in place as per the normal progression of things. The only thing that had really changed was that I was no longer physically the same; yet I still had dreams and desires I wanted to fulfill; college was at the top of the list.

The transition to college isn't easy no matter where you come from. You leave the senior high school big shot behind when you arrive at college as a meager freshman. Just like the first day in any new school, you feel like you stick out, and your nerves are pushed to the limit. There are many adjustments to be made, including upperclassmen to deal with and professors determined to challenge your limits. Since I went to a county junior college in Dallas, my initial transition was not that bad. The physical layout of the buildings meant longer distances between classes. That first semester, I really built up my strength just getting to class. Classes were also tougher, and the workload heavier. Like any freshman, I experienced first day jitters. I had anxiety about finding where my next class was and about having to traverse the campus in between classes. I did not want to be late.

Freshman have that look in their eyes—one of bewilderment that's hard to miss. Being a guy who wanted to be at the top of his game and be prepared, I had to overcome the logistics of things just to make it to class. As a competitive person, I pushed myself to succeed. I wanted and needed to meet new people and to become friends with them. Fortunately, I wasn't the only one in a wheelchair. That helped a great deal with the transition. Anxious to learn and to make a new start, I worked at getting over the football scholarship thing, setting my sights on obtaining a degree. I had to make a living when I got out of school, a big hurdle to jump that would require a great deal of work.

I liked to go to parties, and of course, alcohol was ever-present, and the few times I've overindulged have not been my proudest moments. To say it was something everybody did wasn't the whole story. Drugs were not for me, but alcohol took the edge off— and then some. I guess I behaved the way most college kids do, but there were times I took it too far. Was I anesthetizing myself to keep from dealing with things? That's likely. Coping issues were always present and the challenging new environment added to the mix. I had to find ways to acclimate to the college grind.

Acclimatizing included trying to take notes. College classes being what they are, they require a lot of note-taking. I couldn't do that on my own, so I had to find a notetaker. Using special Xerox paper, I would get a copy of the notes. In the end, it worked OK, but it was hard to follow someone else's notes. My advisor brought up the idea of computers. Actually, it seemed to me that they pushed computers at me a lot. In retrospect, that was probably a good thing since computers have ended up playing a significant role in my life.

I was in liberal arts, studying political science and history. If you remember *Gideon's Trumpet*, the movie I saw the night before my accident, I imagined myself becoming a lawyer. Over time, I'd put a lot of thought into making it into law school, and political science now seemed a good preparatory step. In the field of law, I could apply my analytical skills to solve issues; it seemed like the perfect calling. Yes, there were physical limitations to a certain extent, but my mind was sharp, and I had the desire to achieve. Along with the work, I did find some friends and there were lots of laughs. I used my trademark humor to get through tough situations; it kept things from being too serious or overwhelming. What else can you do but go with the flow?

While I was at community college, me and some of the other guys and girls in wheelchairs started working out together in the gym. Our college hosted a wheelchair sanctioned track and field event, something I didn't even know existed at the time. I went and watched and was hooked. It had all the elements that drew me to football and athletics: pushing yourself to be the best, competition and teamwork, and having others pushing and cheering you on.

One team that really caught my eye was a college team from the University of Texas at Arlington. I spoke briefly with the coach, who also was in a wheelchair. His name was Jim Hays. Coach Hays invited me for a visit to the campus to see what UTA was all about. I went home and told my parents about the invite and a meeting was set. Wheeling onto campus and seeing the layout was a thrill. We met with Coach Hays and he showed me the ropes. The wheelchair track and basketball programs had their own gym. Coach explained he really would like to see me go out for the track team, saying that with my long arms, I should do great in the club throw. The club throw was a wheelchair track event that involved throwing a small, bowling pin like device as far as you could. It was a modified event for those quadriplegics with limited hand function. Coach Hays was firm as to the expectations and demands of a student athlete. If a candidate had what it took, he or she would earn the same athletic letter as non-disabled athletes. He also said that he would make a Super Quad out of me before I graduated! Super Quad was a term given at the time to the higher-level quadriplegics who functioned at a lower level than usual. I thought I had died and gone to heaven, and I told my parents that this was the college for me.

A plan was set in motion for my eventual transfer to UTA. In the meantime, I continued my studies at community college. My friends and I organized our workout together, pushing our wheelchairs around the gym. It was good having friends that looked like me. We were sounding boards for each other and I found it therapeutic to talk. Sometimes I would stay after practice and push around the gym by myself, doing my usual thinking about and analyzing things. I found pushing around the gym to be both peaceful and calming. I thought about my future, and all that had happened in my life.

* * *

Things seemed brighter; I was going to be okay. I went to community college for three semesters, and then it was time for me to move on to UTA. I befriended a guy who was also looking to transfer to UTA. We talked it over and he became my first roommate in college. I'm sure my parents were worried about me moving out of the house and living on my own. When I think back on the courage it took for them to let me go, their role in it all was enormous. The independence I gained by moving away from home made me a better man, and a better person overall.

The University of Texas at Arlington was a whole new world, and thankfully, it wasn't all work. I spent some time wheeling with the newfound team and a new group of friends I'd met. One guy in particular ended up becoming a lifelong friend, and his name was Ray Cerda. Ray and I hit it off from day one. He was a high school football player in Irving, TX, when a car accident derailed his dreams. He was a C5/6 quadriplegic just like me. UTA had a bar called "The Dry Gulch" in the basement of the student union building. We would go there and drink beer and talk and laugh about things. Ray was the first close friend I had who was also in a wheelchair and boy, we had fun.

Each semester, a group of graduate students would rotate in and help with our wheelchair track team. Their duties included helping with equipment, and transferring each of us into specialized track wheelchairs. It was one of those grad students who caught my eye. Her name was Janet. I noticed how comfortable she always was around our team, as if our wheelchairs had somehow magically disappeared. She saw us as individuals, not seeing the wheelchair first—

a new experience for me. When Janet looked at me, for some reason I didn't see any barriers between us.

I hatched a plan with my best friend Ray. I told Ray I wanted to go out with Janet and take her on a date, just the two of us. He said to just ask her out, but I was nervous. I had dated many girls by this age—even with being in a wheelchair I had little fear of rejection—but this was different for some reason. I know Janet thought Ray and I were crazy because we were always clowning around. I told Ray, "Let's see if Janet will go out to dinner with us after practice", and he agreed. One day, before I had the chance to ask Janet, she said, "Let's all go to dinner on Friday," to which we both said OK. Ray told me that this was my chance ... I would show up for a date, telling Janet that Ray wasn't feeling well and couldn't make it. "The rest is up to you, buddy," he said. I was nervous as hell, as you might imagine. I pulled up to the gym where we had all agreed to meet before going to the restaurant. "Where's Ray?" she asked with a smile.

"Oh, he was not feeling well and couldn't make it. I thought we could go."

"Great!" she said.

"Do you like Mexican food?" I asked.

"Sure, nice and spicy." We went to a nice place called Marion's, a little bit fancier than your typical family restaurant. By this time, it was feeling more like a date than a get-together. We had a great time and agreed to go out again.

After that first date, we started to see each other more and more. You know, I've always been a worrier to a certain extent, worrying about the future and what could happen. With that mindset, I tended to overthink things and anticipate events even though they might not materialize. Janet was just the opposite. She lived in the moment and enjoyed every bit of it. To her, the future was off in the distance, something about which she didn't worry. As a result, her disposition was more cheerful, and she relished the moment in which she found herself. With my way of looking at things, I often had a cloud of concern hanging over me, leaving me unable to truly enjoy the present moment because there was always that *what if* lurking just around the corner. We balanced each other out and became good friends, so much so that I wanted to marry her. Janet was studying to work with children with disabilities; she had a huge heart and she embraced the world, especially where kids were concerned.

I'll admit that thinking about marriage was a giant leap for a guy in a wheelchair. Yet, even in the wheelchair, I still had the same aspirations as most of the guys my age; marrying, settling down, and having kids were things I wanted to do. Understanding the enormous obstacles we faced caused my analytical side to kick in, but living in the moment as she did, Janet couldn't see a problem with us getting married. I had worries about saddling her with my issues, and I had definite concerns about Janet taking on so much responsibility within our marriage. There was the matter of children, for instance. How would we have kids?

When love finds you, you don't want to let it go; we both decided to go forward. For us, the decision was relatively easy. My self-esteem increased, and for someone who overanalyzed things, the future appeared bright. However, that optimism was short-lived. From the outset, many people were against the marriage, especially on Janet's side of things. As if it were something easy to dismiss, we were advised to put the notion out of our heads, just like that—that was the gist of it, anyway. But what about our hearts? Mind over matter doesn't always work, and I'm not sure in this case if it ever should.

When you give your heart to someone, you take a chance—a big one. You risk having your heart broken. Still, isn't that what love is about? Aren't we supposed to take risks when we look for love? You must put yourself out there and put everything on the line. Hopefully, that's the case with the people with whom we fall in love ... We both take the leap of faith. We should give ourselves to one another completely, trusting that it will work out. In essence, we want to spend our lives loving and taking care of each other.

Granted, in Janet's case, the majority of the burden would land squarely on her, and I think her family and friends considered that too much of a burden. Was she wasting her life with a guy like me? Maybe so. At first, that was a tough pill to swallow. Under the circumstances, I could understand, to a degree, how the naysayers felt. Nevertheless, I thought I was better than what they thought. I knew that I could give Janet a good life, and love her the way she deserved to be loved. And oh, how I loved her! Sure, it would be difficult, but most worthwhile things are difficult to achieve. We had a lot going for us despite my physical limitations. From the outside looking in, there would always be an imbalance in the relationship, and Janet would need to sacrifice a great deal to be married to me. Being on the inside, and still being realistic, Janet and I thought we could make it. It was worth a try.

I can see how Janet's friends and family thought that she was taking too big of a risk on someone like me. She was told she'd be a caregiver the rest of her life. We both heard secondhand that our marriage wouldn't last a year. Janet was hurt terribly when she was told she was wasting her life; I was hurt too. Words like that stick in your craw and they break your heart. They give you tough things to think about, and open doors to painful perspectives. We were both in distress, but Janet was undeterred. She was headstrong, and wouldn't let a few naysayers derail our dreams. We went ahead and planned our wedding. Janet's parents, for whom I had a lot of respect, did come around somewhat, and they helped Janet plan an outdoor ceremony at their home.

It came to the point in the planning where we needed to pick someone to officiate, someone to read our vows and join us together in marriage. Janet knew just the minister for the job—someone who had been a longtime family friend and whose sister was, in fact, Janet's namesake. So she went to see her Episcopalian minister. Who better than a minister to help us in our quest? That's what we both thought. Surely, he would be a man of reason, understanding of what we wanted to do and that we truly loved one another.

With love how can you fail? Janet had a great deal of respect for this man and as such, valued his opinion. To me, he was a glimmer of hope, the potential voice of reason we needed to assuage family and friends that we could do this thing. We could get married and live happy and fulfilled lives. A minister is experienced in counseling people in their trials and tribulations. He knows that "Love is patient. Love is kind," and he should know that of "faith, hope and love, the greatest of these is love." Janet's hopes were quickly dashed. The minister listened to her, and then responded that he wouldn't marry us because I was in a wheelchair! I would first have to prove that I could have children.

Janet was devastated. Here was a man she had respected for years dealing both her and me a horrible blow. It was a gut punch, the kind that lingers, bruising the mind and breaking the heart. Some things are just too much to forget and too much to get over. However, Janet's reaction and response was one of pure resilience. "You know," she said to me, "it's really none of his business what we do when the lights go out. Our choice of who marries us is ours, and ours alone." We found someone else who was more than happy to marry us and who clearly saw the love and commitment we had (and still have) for each other. In the end, I think it worked out better. He was the same man who later officiated over the funeral of both of Janet's parents. It's strange how life works out that way.

CHAPTER 16

The lead up to our marriage was a stressful period for Janet. She was trying to finish up her graduate program as well as plan the wedding. For me, the whole affair naturally made me reflective. I didn't want to see her hurt; I didn't want to get hurt either. We had our distractors and skeptics, but we also had friends and family who were genuinely happy for us. The planning and excitement were building, and the day finally came in late August of 1988. The evening was perfect, and frankly, the turnout was much larger than I expected. Janet was as beautiful as ever. Sadly, Randy, my close childhood friend, was not able to attend. He had joined the Army after college and had commitments. Our vows were exchanged, and we embarked on our odyssey together as a couple. Janet and I took a leap of faith, and we survived.

I look back on that day some thirty-plus years ago and wonder how I got here: the fear, disappointment, setbacks, failures … How have I survived all I've gone through? There is no control and structure with regard to life. We are living in a pinball machine and we humans are the ball. Each time I get slapped by the flipper paddles, I do my best to bounce back, somehow finding the courage to carry on. I've been asked more than a few times: "Where does that resilience come from?" I must give my parents a lot of credit for how they guided me, especially after the accident. They didn't try to change me; rather, they encouraged me to be me. My parents could have tied me down and babied me, but they didn't. They had the courage to let me fly and to stretch my wings.

Their support and guidance gave me the confidence I needed to strike out on my own. By age eighteen or nineteen, I was on my own, making decisions, and my own mistakes. That's the way it should be. I've known people in my set of circumstances who were really tied down by parents who wouldn't let them do anything. In the end, that approach fosters a dependency that can make a disability or physical challenge worse. Just because we can't often do things for ourselves doesn't mean we've reverted to being helpless children. I think parents of children who've suffered a serious injury sometimes feel they need to wrap their child up in a security blanket or armor so they don't get hurt again. Some parents can't deal with the guilt, or can't handle seeing their kids suffer — it can become a control issue. But when a person has reached a certain age, he or she wants and needs to live their own life, however things work out. At least, they must be given a chance to try and do that.

I'm very grateful my parents supported me in living life the way I wanted to live it. Growing up, I was never excused from my responsibilities. That helped me when it came time for college, and then a career. You don't get a free pass in life, and once you dive into the adult world of having to provide for yourself, you must face the day's challenges and get on with it. Sure, there are days you'd like to play hooky or call in sick, but you must tough it out. No, it's not easy, but if you do keep going, facing the day and all that goes with it, by the end of the day you have earned a sense of accomplishment. When you go to bed, you know you did your best; you didn't try to duck out on the tough stuff. Sleep comes easier.

I have had people comment to me over the years that they don't know how they would have responded to a similar accident if it had happened to them. They suspect that they would not be able to handle the life altering transformation from able-bodied to disabled. In reply, I tell them not to underestimate what can be accomplished. As humans, we have the power to shape the future and the kind of lives we live by the choices

236

we make—that's not to say it won't be hard or that everyone starts with a level playing field—but we can work to shape our destiny. I was fortunate in so many ways with the roads my choices led me down, and for that, I am forever grateful.

The first three years of our marriage went off without much of a hitch; I think you call it the honeymoon phase. We went on trips and pretty much acted like every other couple. I won't say we didn't have our share of disagreements, but nothing that seemed out of the ordinary. Every new couple has that settling in phase. We both agreed that in about three to five years, we would look at starting a family one way or another. Frankly, doctors had told me that they weren't sure if I could have kids naturally. As we put those plans on hold, little did we know that we were about to be challenged in a big way.

CHAPTER 17

As I've said, when we first got married, Janet and I wanted to wait to see about having kids, and we didn't even know if it would be possible. We just wanted to get through the early stages of marriage to see if we would make it. Turns out, we did fine. It was about this time that Janet and I had heard about help for people with spinal cord injuries who wanted to have kids. Apparently, a new procedure was available. Janet was seven years older than me and time for her to have children was limited; we decided to investigate.

The procedure involved electro-ejaculation and depended on synchronization with Janet's ovulation times to ensure optimum timing. My sperm count had to be checked, along with motility and mobility: everything looked good. Then, a fickle thing called "fate" stepped in, and not in a good way. Here, my grandmother's words about complacency come to mind. Let's just say that things got in the way. I still had a lingering fear of hospitals (a fear that has remained with me to this day). For me, going to the hospital is like a PTSD nightmare: I just can't get past the dread I have felt ever since my accident. Coming down with something, or simply not feeling well can cause me some anxiety; if I get really sick, it's even worse.

So, when I began to feel unwell, I tried to slough it off as just the flu, or something mundane. I really didn't want to contemplate anything serious. I was running a bit of a fever, but didn't think much of it. By the second day, I still wasn't feeling any better, and in fact, I felt a little worse. Janet stayed home from work to be with me. By day three, I still wasn't feeling better. I went to my family doctor, who thought I had a bladder infection. The problem with spinal injuries is that you don't experience much sensation below the injury line. It's impossible to know if something hurts. Since bladder infections are common, the doctor just assumed that was the issue.

We agreed with the diagnosis and the doctor prescribed some antibiotics. I went home and took them, but still wasn't doing any better. Two days later, Janet said she thought I needed to go to the emergency room. That was the last place I wanted to go and I told her I wasn't going. The memory of the accident and the months in the hospital were still very fresh in my mind. *No*, I wasn't going anywhere. By the following night, my fever had shot up and I was drifting in and out of consciousness. Finally, I couldn't take any more. About midnight, I told Janet that I had to get to the hospital. Fears and all, I knew that something was horribly wrong and I needed to go. I had to have a neighbor come and load me in his truck. Off we went!

The doctors ordered a CT scan and saw that I had an abscessed appendix. As a result, I had a bad infection. Yup—I really should have listened to Janet and gone to the hospital sooner. I was still drifting in and out of consciousness. My parents came to see me in the hospital, and I told them I didn't think I was going to make it. My dad was furious with the hospital staff because I'd been admitted on Friday and they hadn't done anything for me all weekend. However, by Monday night, I was wheeled into surgery. I was told I had a twenty percent chance of survival.

When the surgeon got in there, he found the worst case of an abscessed appendix he'd ever seen. On top of that, the tissue had become dangerously gangrenous. Several feet of my intestine had to be removed. Talk about being in bad shape!

My dad's side of the family has a history of appendicitis, and it used to be a common cause of death in rural areas because people couldn't get into town soon enough for help. Once the appendix ruptures or gets infected, that infection spreads. It's usually fatal. I didn't have the excuse of living in a rural area—my fears had kept me away from the hospital—perhaps at an even greater distance than folks living in the country. It was a tough lesson learned. One of the sad things was that I had been recently hired to work with an executive director of a non-profit organization. Well, I was in the hospital for three months! I had drainage tubes in me to handle the pockets of infection, and then my lungs filled up with fluid. At one point, they thought I had spinal meningitis. My system underwent a whole cadre of problems.

Drained from the relentless fever and still drifting in and out of consciousness, I would occasionally come to and find my room filled with people who wanted to do this or that procedure. One day, I'd finally had enough and threw everyone out. I asked for my dad, and the doctor. When the doctor arrived, I asked him point blank if I was going to die. At twenty-five, I didn't yet have a will—I didn't have anything—and I wasn't prepared to die. Janet would be left with all sorts of issues to deal with alone, and I didn't want that for her. The doctor's answer was that I had fluid building up in my lungs, and that I was in a tough spot. The decision was made to put me in a chill bed to manage the fever.

Janet had to keep working. We needed to keep her salary coming in and my insurance was with her employer. I didn't want her to lose her job because she wanted to be at the hospital. My parents were able to be with me, right by my side, and so Janet kept on working.

I hadn't slept in days. That, combined with the medication, gave me hallucinations. It was horrible. Janet and I hadn't been married that long and we were still in the discovery stage with one another; I'm glad my dad was there so that Janet didn't have to go through that.

I lost my job, and that was tough. The non-profit company had no provisions for disability pay. Overall, the recovery process took about a year. You'd think after the accident I would be used to long recovery periods, but no, not at all. I had lost a lot of muscle and strength, and I found myself back at the proverbial square one. I could hardly get around in my wheelchair; I was far too weak. What a recovery period! It was so frustrating, but I got through it one day at a time.

After that grueling period in our lives, I believe that Janet and I emerged stronger. We both felt it was time to once again try for a family. We started fertility treatments and finally, in the spring of 1993, Janet conceived. Her pregnancy was not a smooth one. From the first ultrasound, we found out we were having twins! I thought I was going to fall out of my wheelchair. (Twins happened to run on Janet's side of the family). Several weeks into her pregnancy, the doctor ordered her on bed rest. One morning, while my attendant was helping me in the shower, Janet came in and said she thought her water had broken while in the bathroom. The thought came in my head that it was way too early and I was scared, but tried not to show it. We were both scared, but given all we had been through to this point in our lives, we held it together.

We raced to the hospital and our fears were confirmed as Janet was rushed in for an emergency C-section. Our twins, a boy and a girl, were born two months premature in early November 1993. When babies are born prematurely, they can have all kinds of issues, such as breathing and heart problems, brain and eyesight problems, intestinal problems, and so on. It was a frightening time for us. Looking at those tiny babies, a wave of emotions hit me. We didn't want to lose them! I told them that I would be the best father I could be, and that they needed to fight to survive.

One morning, we came to visit them on our daily vigil to the neonatal ICU. The nurse stopped us and asked if we would wait in one of the conference rooms for the doctor. Both our hearts sank, knowing the news was bad. We had seen other couples emerge from this room and the look of heartbreak was obvious. I tried to prepare for the news as best I could, but Janet's sobs were unbearable. I started to tear up and we embraced each other as we waited. I was not used to this feeling of being on the other side of the curtain, so to speak. I was usually the one in bad health situations, struggling to survive, and now the shoe was on the other foot. It felt terrible.

As the doctor came in, he was composed and direct. He had done this many times in his career, I was sure, and was desensitized to the news he had to deliver. "I want to inform you, Mr. and Mrs. Wallgren, that your son is probably not going to make it. He has a virus, and he is very sick. You need to prepare for this the best you can. Do you have any questions?"

Janet asked if we could see our son, and the doctor agreed. As I wheeled into the room, I could tell he was struggling to survive. His skin color had changed and tubes had been inserted in veins I never thought possible. I remember looking at him, then glancing over at my daughter not far away and thinking: *What I have done to deserve this pain?* My rational, analytical brain was spinning like a magnet held closely to a compass. The situation was out of my control and there wasn't a damn thing I could do about it. I could no more stop what was about to happen than I could stop the wind from blowing. Given that, I was not a man of faith ... I simply had to let the events unfold and do the best I can. I had to accept the fact that when we are born, nothing is given, nothing is promised, and nothing is predetermined. I could only control how I responded.

Not fully ready to give up, I placed my hand on my son and told him I loved him and that I would see him soon. I wiped the tears and left the room, fully expecting to never see him again. We left the hospital, driving home in utter silence. This was before the days of cell phones, and we wanted to be home in case the hospital called. The call never came, but the effects of that experience have never left me, nor Janet.

Eventually, the twins pulled through and were fine. The hospital bills were gargantuan, so I'm glad we had insurance. Even so, the bills were close to a quarter of a million dollars. Watching your children lying in incubators during their struggle makes a parent forget all about other troubles; all our focus was on the babies. I'm grateful that they pulled through, turning into wonderful kids, and eventually, fine adults. They are caring, considerate, and compassionate— all a father could ask for in his children.

Having the kids presented new challenges for me. Restricted hand movement made holding them difficult, and as they started to grow, I wondered about how they'd view me in a wheelchair. I missed much in their lives due to my limitations: roller coaster rides, and cave exploring, and kids teased them because I was different. Physically, I couldn't be like other fathers.

How would I toss a football to my son or daughter? Would I even want to have my son play football? I had some big questions for which I didn't have immediate answers, and many things had to be considered. Each parent wants their children to have things, to do things, and to be happy and healthy—I was no exception. It was important for me to be active in my kids' lives and to be there for them, so I found ways to do that. When I wasn't working, I could drive them to school, and go to their games.

The issue about my son or perhaps my daughter playing football had been in the back of my mind for years. As my son got older, I wasn't sure how to handle it, but it turned out that it was never an issue because he was naturally more into music than sports. That was fine; however, I was still left with the dilemma about whether kids should play football. Even today, parents come up to me and ask me if they should let their sons play football: great question!

I still watch and love the game and what happened to me was an accident. Could it happen to others? Yes, and it has many times. I guess it comes down to one thing: Is the risk worth it? I was a gung-ho kid, diving into just about everything I tried. My life did take a mighty turn away from my goals, so yes, I have regrets, but it just meant that I had to create new goals. Were they choices I would have made if the accident hadn't happened? Probably not; however, human beings can adapt to new situations and thrive. I certainly did, although at times, it seemed impossible. I ended up being able to overcome my physical limitations, my mental blocks, and most of my fears. I finished high school, graduated from college, got married, and had twins! I'm proud of that; I'm proud of my family.

Growing up, I never dreamed that my life would take a dramatic detour, yet any of us could be faced with the same thing. Life can change in a heartbeat, and if a person lives long enough, he or she will most likely face many challenges. No doubt, if I had known what would happen, I might have opted out. But I'm a risk taker (to an extent) and I put myself out there. Challenges have always motivated me. To me, you must use challenges as motivation to overcome obstacles in your life. If you give in … if you quit trying to succeed, you've lost more than you realize.

We all have trials to get through. Some people have physical trials, others have emotional or mental challenges, and many of us have financial struggles; some people deal with a combination of those issues. Ultimately, it's *how* we deal with our struggles that will either help, or hurt us. Endeavor to keep a positive attitude. Learn from your mistakes, and don't be afraid of failure. By always going forward, always trying to improve yourself and your situation, you shape the way in which your brain works, and assist your body in building the much needed strength to overcome adversity.

It's true that we don't know how strong we are until we're put to the test. We don't know what we can do unless we're tried, sometimes by fire. Embracing the situation, even the bad stuff, will help us to overcome the worst, and give us the strength to live the best way we can.

My wife, my parents, my kids, siblings, and friends have certainly been instrumental in helping me live life to the fullest. It's not what I imagined, but it's been a great life. To each of them and to all of them, I give them my love and thanks!

CHAPTER 18

In 2016, statistics showed that sixty-eight percent of all football injuries occur during tackles. Kids participating in high school sports are at risk for injury, but by far, the majority of injuries involve players who participate in football. Most of the injuries are to the head and face; however, with modern medical technology and prevention programs in place, the frequency and seriousness of the injuries are declining.

It has long been known—and recent studies concur—that participation in school sports is good for students. In fact, kids who participate in sports have higher GPAs (Grade Point Averages) and are more disciplined than students who do not participate. The rigorous physical exertion common in sports is good for the body and the mind. Kids who are active in sports have a much better outlook on life and have fewer problems with self-esteem. Furthermore, people who participate in sports go on to be great team players in the business sector. Employers find that those individuals have the "stick-to-itness" so necessary in the workplace.

When I was participating in sports, about four million students across the country were active in some sort of high school sport. Now, that number has doubled. Programs designed to prevent sports injuries have also grown. One important such program is the Program for Injury Prevention, Education and Research (PIPER) in Colorado. Athletic directors from all over the country supply the program with statistics, which are detailed in a yearly report. The report indicates that there are approximately 500,000 injuries in sports every year—a significant number. According to reports, only ten percent of those injuries required surgery. While that statistic is encouraging, the report also indicated that eleven high school football players had died in 2015: that's eleven too many. Nevertheless, players now are better trained, and can withstand injury better than kids of my generation could do.

Athletic trainers are also more abundant on football teams, but their representation is low nationwide. Schools that do have trainers in place are able to keep the number of sports injuries down; sadly, only thirty-seven percent of teams have trainers on staff. It's not always the tackles in football that can cause harm— often, the effects of heat and dehydration can be a bad combination. Two-a-day practices increase the risk factor because there is more stress placed on the athletes.

Ivy League schools have banned tackling during practices and the NCAA has restricted tackling to just two practices per week. My accident didn't occur during a game, but rather in practice, so these new restrictions are a good thing!

Coaches have stepped up as well, and many have revised their coaching to include an emphasis on preventing injuries. Hopefully, the days of teaching kids to knock someone's block off are gone. Parents also have a responsibility in terms of monitoring their children's sports activities. They need to check out the individual programs to find out if safety is a key component. How do the coaches handle their teams? Is there disregard for the athletes' safety? Is there an athletic trainer and/or a doctor present during practices and games?

A critical factor that often never hits the radar are the number of injuries that happen after half-time. Obviously, players' bodies cool down during half-time, which adds risk. Now, some schools are adding warm-ups right before the third quarter to reduce potential injury from a sudden cool down. They use stretching and other warm-up exercises to prepare the athletes to hit the field again. This is a new concept and one that should also reduce injuries. Studies to test this concept have been conducted using a control group who did not warm up after half-time, and another group who did. Teams implementing the warm-ups had significantly fewer injuries in the third quarter!

It's also worth noting that artificial turf is proven to cause more injuries than natural turf. Many high schools don't have artificial turf, but some do, and as a result, injuries are more plentiful.

Back when I was in high school football, a study was conducted in Birmingham, Alabama on high school football injuries. Covering the period from 1976 to 1979, a total of 1877 injuries were reported from 661 games and 1216 practices. Those injuries were treated at the Sports Medicine Clinic at the University of Alabama. Of those injuries, 7.6 percent affected the head and neck. When I was playing football, the tackling method of "spearing" was still widely in use. That's tackling an opponent with your head in the lead. Now, spearing is prohibited. Even so, the number of athletes paralyzed per year in football averages between twenty-five and thirty.

The numeric toll of severe injuries doesn't really indicate how many family members suffer due to those injuries. A disabling injury isn't just felt and dealt with by the player: there's a ripple effect that happens— believe me, I know. I definitely wasn't the only one to feel the repercussions of that tackle that day at practice. My family suffered the consequences along with me, something that doesn't change with time.

The consequences of serious injury go beyond the emotional, psychological, and physical aspects. Many of football's devastating injuries result in enormous medical bills. Yes, insurance can cover a good portion of them, but there are many things insurance doesn't cover. The residual bills can destroy a family's financial well-being. Those medical costs continue throughout life, depending on the severity of the injuries. In my case, ancillary health issues will always be there. The daily expenses of maintaining the injured person's health mount up. Cars and homes must be adapted to accommodate disabilities; attrition and age also contribute to financial woes.

So, given all of that, what do the recent stats about high school football players show? To be accurate, we must put things in perspective. During the 2018 to 2019 football season, 1,006,013 kids participated in high school football. If you look at the relative number of injuries that occurred, the statistics are remarkably low. Last year was the twentieth year in which over one million kids participated in high school football.

Injuries notwithstanding, participation in the sport is still high. Even so, boys and girls have discussions with their moms, just like I did, often pleading for permission to play football. My mother caved in and I'm sure she regretted that decision; I have mixed emotions. Obviously, I was excited to play, and at the time, it was great because my mom gave me the okay. As things turned out, her protective instincts were valid, but neither of us could have foreseen the accident that altered my life forever.

I can't recommend whether a child should participate in football or not—that's a parent's decision to make. Things happen all the time, and not just in sports. For example, we usually get keys to the car when we're sixteen, and car crashes can occur. The fact is that accidents do happen; it's all a part of life. What's the answer then? In weighing the pros and cons, it appears that advances have been made since my accident to make the sport safer; however, we still see the blowback from football veterans suffering from Parkinson's, Alzheimer's, and dementia, plus other significant side effects from football.

My friend, Steve, from the hospital, had a pool injury. Should that cause us to avoid swimming and diving? The fact is that we all have choices to make in life each day and it's not always conducive to mental health to be constantly afraid that things will go wrong. Yes, we should be prudent and make informed decisions, but accidents are just that: they're unforeseeable twists of fate. Afterwards, we can second guess our decisions—I've done that. I've looked at things backwards and forwards, right-side up and upside down in an effort to understand and still come up short.

My counterpart on the football field that day hit me hard, and I hit him hard. He walked away, and I never walked again. Things might have been just the opposite or we both might have been hurt. The truth is that football can be dangerous; life is dangerous. A decision to send your kid into dangerous situations is normally not something parents would do. In my case, I was headstrong and I wanted to play. I look at it as my decision to play football, and mine alone. The simple fact that I was in the play when I got hurt was due to my choice to participate. I raised my hand, had my helmet on, and jogged onto the field. I hold no one responsible—the consequences fall squarely on my shoulders.

In thinking about the ironies of life, Steve sticks in my mind. He went through rehab and learned to drive. He made a life for himself. His disability took a toll on his marriage, which sadly ended up in divorce, but he went on with his life. On a cold Austin, Texas night, with a light dusting of snow and ice, he drove up to his house. His medical attendant was inside. Steve was exiting his van in his power wheelchair when he got stuck on the slick ice. It was the pre-cellphone era. He must have yelled for help, but no one heard him. His attendant had fallen asleep on the couch. The next morning, Steve was found by a neighbor; he'd frozen to death. Steve couldn't have foreseen the situation; it was an accident. The simple fact is that when you put yourself out there and try to live your life, stuff happens. So, what do we do? We keep on living, that's what. We keep on trying. My life changed dramatically and still has its highs and lows. Like anyone's life, it certainly has its challenges, but nevertheless, I'm grateful for the life I've lived.

Have I ever thought about ending it all? Sadly, at one point, I did. When I think of all I would have missed, I look back and wonder why I even thought of suicide. Life is a day to day thing, one moment after another. Those moments may be embraced, ignored, or hated, but they are the building blocks of a life.

Surprises have been abundant in my life, both good and bad, but I'm still here, still trying, still living, and still wondering about things. Am I more cautious now? I think I'm more prudent. Maybe that comes with age or experience—more likely with both. It's hard to say what my life would have been like without the accident. I only know the life I've lived following the accident has a beauty all its own. We all have regrets, but the detours in my life have given me a whole new perspective.

Who knows the real reason things happen? That's something we probably won't understand on this side of the grave. And perhaps that's okay. Not everything can be understood; not every piece of the puzzle can be found. It's the search for the answers that propels us on a journey towards tomorrow, a tomorrow filled with its own joys, and its own sorrows, but also happiness and peace.

If I hadn't learned in sports to keep trying, to keep pushing myself to be better, I might not have developed the skills I needed to live my life and to overcome powerful challenges. Without sports, without a competitive nature, I might have acquiesced and never experienced marriage and kids. Regardless of the accident, I'm blessed. Life can be wonderful, but like football, it's a contact sport. We've got to get in there, and play for keeps.

Ray Cerda, Janet and Jim in 1987

Last Picture of me before accident March 1980

Best friend Randy at his wedding 1992

Janet and Jim 1988

Janet, John, Jim, Aubrey Wallgren

Mom and Dad

Kindness by Jim Wallgren
09/21/2010

(This is a poem the author wrote and presented to Mac
Davis when they met)

If I could write a song I am not sure what I would say.

About a man and his guitar and how are paths crossed
that day.

The story should be told, for it's my story to tell.

About a boy all of 15 and his impending hell.

My body has left me and in its void replaced by fear.

My mind drifts and frolics in those healthy years.

I struggle to stay positive and to keep my mind sain.

Please tell me how to deal with this pain.

It's funny how despair can change on a dime.

In a smile or glance or across a telephone line.

A reassuring voice to confirm all will be OK.

To give a boy a little hope and brighten up his day.

The case is beat up and torn many travels I am sure.

A guitar and a note, with a sound so pure.

It's brought me good luck kid and I know she has a few more.

PS "Don't Sell It", for I'm sure he would be sore

Thirty years have past and if my mind starts to wonder it makes me weep.

But, I have lived a full life and my wife, kids and family they makes it complete.

It's time to start a new chapter and to close this door.

This old guitar has brought me good luck and I know she has some more.

If I could write a song I do know what I would say.

Random acts of kindness make this world a better place.

A Note From The Author's Wife

Life with someone who uses a wheelchair to access his environment is not much different than someone who doesn't use one.

There are struggles and of course joys with both in any marriage.

When Jim and I got engaged, many of our family and friends were against the marriage from the start. It did bother me some but when you love someone you just go ahead and do what you feel is right; you get married.

I helped Jim and his friends during his wheelchair track practice and I never saw the chair but just saw the person and how wonderful, fun, and kind he was. We have been married for almost

32 years and have twins who have brightened our life.

We have basically done everything that other people have done from camping in a tent to seeing other parts of the country.

There has been break downs and struggles in some things that we have done, but we have overcome them and become stronger as a couple.

I so admire who you are, Jim, for all that you have done and become even with using a wheelchair for almost 40 years. Keep up the great work and know that I love you.

Janet

A Note From The Author's Daughter

It's hard writing about my dad. I've known no other dad in the world, and if you ask me to tell you what makes my dad different from anyone else, I wouldn't say "well he's in a wheelchair".

In fact, this is something I often forget to tell people because him being in a wheelchair isn't a defining feature about it; it's not something that I feel I have to mention to everyone in my life.

What I would tell you that he's funny. I remember him rapping in the car when taking my best friend and I somewhere, and how he used to tell my brother and I to go to bed at 1pm in the afternoon.

I would tell you that he's smart. You could ask him anything, and 9/10, he has an answer. It might not be the right answer, but hey, he tried. He has strong opinions about certain things, but he always backs it up with facts. Every time I talk to him, I would swear he has something new to tell me. It seems that he's always learning, and I love that about him.

I would also tell you that he's loving. He loves his wife, his kids, and his whole family. He and my mother taught me how important family is, and how to grow up with people who love and care about you The last thing I'd tell you about my dad is that he taught me, alongside my mom, to be caring and kind. To never judge a book by it's cover. To do what brings you the most happiness. They have been right by my side, whether I wanted them there or not, and showed me that they will always support me, and that's all I need in my life.

Aubrey Wallgen

A Note from the Author's Son

D ad's a great father! It was always the best to find ways to play with him as a kid. I remember wearing my roller blades and holding onto his chair while he went up and down the driveway.

He'd also come into our rooms and tell us to go do homework and go to bed at 3 pm.

He's the best father in the world. He's kind, and super smart.

When you get him talking about HAM radios it's hard to keep up with the conversation! He loves his wife, his two beautiful angel children, and the rest of his amazing family.

Love You,

John

A Note from the Author's Parents

James, as we look at all the challenges you have to make from coping with everyday normal problems, to adjustments in your everyday life, it has made you and your family stronger, more patient, understanding, loving and determined.

When you were growing up you had a special way about you.

Even in middle school you seemed more mature for a boy just

13 years old. The teacher even noticed how patient and understanding you were with the other students and friends. We always thought it was because you were so close to your grandparents and their teachings with

your visits to the farm and visits in the summers. You learned a lot a from them.

We cannot find words to tell you how proud we are of you and how you have handled your accident. We have seen you sometimes (a little) depressed but it never got the best of you, it seemed to make you stronger and more determined.

Over the years we look back and think how did James and all of us handle all of the adjustments we have endured. I guess we take it one day at a time... We love you so very much, James...

Love you, Mom and Dad